THE

WARM-UP

PROPER WARM UP & COOL DOWN PROCEDURES

Proper warm-up is critical to the success of the track and field athlete. If done properly, the warm-up will reduce injuries, increase flexibility and ensure the athlete is ready for a great workout.

By following the type of warm-up that you see on the following pages, your athletes will increase their "core" body temperature, which will ensure that all muscle groups are ready for a great track and field workout.

If this type of warm-up is followed, the athlete will still be able to do a high quality workout even if the temperature outside on the track is below 40 degrees. The athlete has now raised their "core" body temperature by doing this type of complete warm-up procedure.

Since you will be training for months, it is critical that you do both your warm up and cool down on grass inside the track or on field turf. Extra pounding on the track for both their warm-up and cool down will increase their chance for injury.

Not cooling down properly will allow you to have serious lactic acid in your body for several days. This cool-down should consist of jogging or walking at least 800 meters after the conclusion of the workout.

Also spending 5-10 minutes of extra time on flexibility after the workout will help in speeding up recovery from your intense workout.

I suggest that your athlete stop by the training room and get a bag of ice and strap it on the middle of the lower back area with some cellophane wrap or tape for at least 15-20 minutes on their way home from school. This will help reduce soreness and swelling of that particular muscle group.

Studies have also shown that if the athlete takes a small bag of ice after practice and places it on the lower part of the back for a period of 15-20 minutes, it will help to reduce any type of muscle inflammation in the legs as the nerves that run down thru the spine to the legs.

Recent studies shows that if an athlete consumes some type of "PROTEIN" within 45 minutes of the actual workout, it will go directly to the muscles that were strained or excessively used during training. After this 45 minute period, you will get less benefit.

Phosphate Plus is a "legal" supplement that will aid in lactic acid flush out, reduce muscle soreness and cramps. This is equivalent to eating 8-9 bananas a day!

If you are running at a park or on the roads, stay off the concrete sidewalks. This will prevent stress fractures and shin splints.

Athletes do not get hurt running on good, quality grass surfaces! The great Coach John McDonnell, former Head Track and Field Coach at the University of Arkansas who won 42 NCAA Championships in Track & Field, spends about a 3-4 week period after the NCAA Indoor Championships in mid-March training on grass. This means Coach McDonnell will take all of his middle and long distance runners out to the cross country course to do the track intervals, distance run's and even their steeplechase hurdling. They will stay on the grass up to the second week of April.

A great "legal" supplement to prevent stress fractures is *Osteo-Tech* which is a "special" Calcium/Magnesium blended formula.

If you would like to read more about these "Legal" supplements, go to **SSEproducts.com** for *Phosphate Plus & Osteo-Tech information or ordering.*

STANDARD WARM-UP PROCEDURE

1. Warm-Up Jog
   - a. 100/200/110 Hurdles   (800 to 1,200 Meters)
   - b. 400 Meters/300 Hurdlers   (1,200 to 1,600 Meters)
   - c. 800 Meters   (1,200 to 2,000 Meters)
   - d. Distance   (1,600 to 2,000 Meters)

2. Static Stretching (10 Minutes)
or

Use of Stretch-Rite Belt (10 Minutes)

3. Dynamic Flexibility Drills (Refer to Chart)

4. Hurdle Rhythm Drills
   - a. Side Skips
   - b. Hurdle Walk-Overs (Hand's on Head)
   - c. Over Hurdle/Under Hurdles
   - d. "A" Skips
   - e. "B" Skips
   - **f.** "C" Skips

5. Speed/Sprint Drills (Refer to Drill Chart)

6. Stride Build-Ups (5 x 60 meters)
   - a. 1 x 60 meters (60%)
   - b. 1 x 60 meters (70%)
   - c. 1 x 60 meters (80%)
   - d. 1 x 60 meters (90%)
   - e. 1 x 60 meters (95%)

"Your Last Stride should be as FAST as anything you will do in the entire workout or track & field meet"

DYNAMIC FLEXIBILITY DRILLS

MONDAY/THURSDAY/SATURDAYS

8 Leg Swings (back & forth)	Right/Left Leg
8 Leg Swings (side to side)	Right/Left Leg
8 Trail Leg-Hip Circles	Right/Left Leg
8 Bicycles	Right/Left Leg
8 Sagital Scissors (side to side)	Right/Left Leg
8 Inverted Scissors (front and back)	Right/Left Leg
8 Abductor/Adductor Straight Leg Raises	Right/Left Leg
8 Single Leg Donkey Kicks	Right/Left Leg
8 Eagles	Right/Left Leg
8 Stomach Eagles	Right/Left Leg
8 Lung Walks	Right/Left Leg

TUESDAY/FRIDAYS

8 Leg Swings (back& forth)	Right/Left Leg
8 Leg Swings (side to side)	Right/Left Leg
8 Trail Hip Circles	Right/Left Leg
8 Bicycles	Right/Left Leg
8 Sagital Scissors (side to side)	Right/Left Leg
8 Inverted Scissors (front & back)	Right/Left Leg
8 Hurdle Seat Leg Pick-ups	Right/Left Leg
8 Hurdle Seat Exchanges	Right/Left Leg
8 Lung Exchanges	Right/Left Leg

WEDNESDAY/SUNDAYS

8 Leg Swings (back& forth)	Right/Left Leg
8 Leg Swings (side to side)	Right/Left Leg
8 Trail Leg Hip Circles	Right/Left Leg
8 Bicycles	Right/Left Leg
8 Sagital Scissors (side to side)	Right/Left Leg
8 Inverted Scissors (back & forth)	Right/Left Leg
8 Russian Cossacks	Right/Left Leg
8 Stomach Eagles	Right/Left Leg
8 Lung Walks	Right/Left Leg

SPEED/SPRINT MECHANICS DRILLS

MONDAY/WEDNESDAY
Side to Side Skips
Slow Motion "Sprint Drill" Technique Drills
Slow "A" Skips
Backward "A" Skips
Single Quick Leg Drill (Right leg)
Single Quick Leg Left (Left leg)
Single Quick Leg Alternators (Right/Left)
Butt Kicks (Knees in front of Body)
Ankling
Straight Leg Bounds/Toe Taps
Fast Active "A" Skips
Quick Feet Drill (Move hand and feet fast for 1 meter)
Acceleration Stick Drills x 5

TUESDAY/THURSDAY/SATURDAYS
Carioca
Slow "A" Skips
"B" Skips
Partner "High Knee" Line Drill
Single Quick Leg (Right Leg)
Single Quick leg   (Left Leg)
Backward Hamstring Run
Power Skips
Butt Kicks
Straight leg Bounds/Toe Taps
Quick Active "A" Skips
Quick Feet Drill (Move hands & feet fast for 1 meter)

FRIDAY/SUNDAY
Side to Side Skips
Slow Motion "Sprint" Drill
Partner "High Knee" Line Drill
Slow "A" Skips
Single Quick Leg Drill (Right Leg)
Single Quick Leg Drill (Left Leg)
Single Quick Leg Alternators (Right/Left)
Butt Kicks (Knees in Front)
Ankling
Straight leg Bounds/Toe Taps
Quick Feet Drill (Move hands and feet fast for 1 meter)
Acceleration Stick Drills X 5

Partner Line Drill

Both athletes get on a line of the track and each athlete face each other. Runner #1 runs fast in place on the middle of the line with high knees and he tries to hit the other Runner #2 hands. Runner #2 purposely walks very slowly backwards with his hands up at chest level. Runner #2 controls the pace and walks the athletes back very slow....

Athlete #1 who is to running fast in place, always tries to keep ½ of his body on each side of the line at all times. If he can not do this then, he must be using "bad" arm mechanics!

I regret that this drill is not in the video!

HURDLE RHYTHM DRILLS

HURDLE SIDE SKIPS	**2 x 5 Hurdles**	(On Side of Each Hurdle)
HURDLE WALK OVERS	**1 x 10 Hurdles**	(Over Top of Hurdle)
OVER UNDERS	**2 x 5 Hurdles**	(Walk Over Top & Then Walk Under Hurdle)
Right Leg "A" Skips	**1 x 10 Hurdles**	
Left Leg "A" Skips	**1 x 10 Hurdles**	
Right Leg "B" Skips	**1 x 10 Hurdles**	
Left Leg "B" Skips	**1 x 10 Hurdles**	
Right Leg "C" Skips	**1 x 10 Hurdles**	
Right Leg "C" Skips	**1 x 10 Hurdles**	

This circuit will help with:

- Coordination
- Rhythm
- Balance
- Strength
- Hip Flexibility
- Strengthens the Hip Flexors

Do 2-3 times a week!

STICK ACCELERATION DRILL

The Stick Acceleration Drill is used by the athlete to help teach gradual acceleration so that the athlete won't hit his maximum acceleration with such a rapid first 20-30 meters. This drill will also teach the athlete not to over-stride during their first 8-10 steps. Over-striding is a common fault in young athletes.

This will also help the athlete to reduce their deceleration period due to a smoother transition from the start/blocks to their maximum acceleration.

OPTIONS
- Paint Marks on Track
- Place Colored Tape on Track
- Wooden Sticks

TRACK MARKINGS
Start to Line 1	50cm
Line 1 to Line 2	65cm
Line 2 to Line 3	80cm
Line 3 to Line 4	95cm
Line 4 to Line 5	110cm
Line 5 to Line 6	125cm
Line 6 to Line 7	140cm
Line 7 to Line 8	155cm

OPTIONAL
STRENGTH
&
POWER
TRAINING
EXERCISES

MULTIPLE SHOT THROWS

BOMB CIRCUIT

Overhead Back Throw	2 Throws
1 Hop onto box Between the Legs Forward	2 Throws
1 Hop on Box Overhead Back	2 Throws
Hammer Throws-Right	1 Throw
Hammer Throws-Left	1 Throw

GUN CIRCUIT

Overhead Back Throw	2 Throws
Between The Legs Forward	2 Throws
Hammer Throw-Right	2 Throws
Hammer Throw-Left	2 Throws

FIRE CRACKER CIRCUIT

Overhead Back Throw	3 Throws
Between The Leg Forward	3 Throws

BODY WEIGHT CIRCUITS

THE BIG BURN

Push-ups	10 Reps
Squat Thrusts	10 Reps
Tread Mills	10 Reps
Frog Jumps	10 Reps
"V" Sit-ups	10 Reps
Donkey Kicks	10 Reps

MEDICINE BALL CIRCUITS

BIG MAMMA CIRCUIT

Chest Pass	2 x 15 Reps
Overhead Pass	2 x 15 Reps
Left Side Throw	2 x 15 Reps
Right Side Throw	2 x 15 Reps
Around The World	2 x 15 Reps
Over-Unders	2 x 15 Reps
Med Ball Sit-ups	2 x 15 Reps

LITTE DUDE CIRCUIT

Chest Pass	2 x 15 Reps
Left Side Throw	2 x 15 Reps
Right Side Throw	2 x 15 Reps
Under Leg Throws	2 x 15 Reps
Med Ball Sit-ups	2 x 15 Reps

<u>What is a Fly?</u>

A fly is an assisted start. These means the athlete gets a 15 to 20 meter running start into the mark that he will take off from. This removes the starting phase from the equation!

Doing a "Fly" helps the athlete reach their top end speed faster. Scientific studies shows by having athletes do fly's from 50 to 100 meters helps the athletes to build their own natural testrone levels without the use of steroids or other banned supplements.

Fly Zone   Timed Distance

Athlete Starts   Timing Starts   Timing Ends

PLYOMETRIC

CIRCUITS

PLYOMETRIC CIRCUITS

Big Sandy (long Jump Pit)

Ankle Jumps	3 x 15 reps
Side to Side	3 x 15 reps
Split Thrust	3 x 15 reps
High Knee Jump Tucks	3 x 15 reps
Frog Hops	3 x 15 reps

Plyo-Jam Circuit (Grass)

Double Leg Hurdle Hops	4 x 10 Reps
Single Leg Bounds-Right Leg	2 x 40 meters
Single Leg Bound Left Leg	2 x 40 meters
Box Circuit	4 x 5 Boxes
Frog Hops for Distance	2 x 10 Hops

Super Ply'o Circuit (Grass)

Double leg Hurdle Hops	5 x 5 Hurdles
Single Leg Bounds (Right Leg)	5 x 40 Meters
Single Leg Bound Left Leg)	5 x 40 Meters
Depth Jumps & Explode Up!	2 x 10 Jumps
On & Off Box Contacts	2 x 10 Jumps

WEIGHT TRAINING EXERCISES

FALL-WEIGHT TRAINING

DAYS: Tuesday & Thursday
Intensity: 80 to 85%

Exercise	Sets	Reps
Hang Cleans	3	10
Hang Snatches	3	10
Bench Press	3	10
Squats	3	10
Surfer Squats	3	10
Speed Squats	3	10
Incline Bench	3	10
Hip Flexor Machine	3	10
Hamstring Curls	3	10
Standing Calves	3	10
Good Mornings	3	10
Step-Ups	3	10
Dumb Bell Lung Walks	3	10
Sit-ups Crunches	3	25
Stadium Stairs	3	50

In Season-Weight Training

Olympic Circuit   Day #1

Hang Cleans	2 x 8 reps
Hang Snatches	2 x 8 reps
Bench Press	2 x 8 reps
Squats	2 x 8 reps
Hip Flexors	2 x 8 reps
Good Mornings	2 x 8 reps
Leg Curls	2 x 8 reps

World Class Circuit Day #2

Split Cleans	2 x 8 reps
Snatches	2 x 8 reps
Bench Press	2 x 8 reps
Speed Squats	2 x 8 reps
Hamstring Curls	2 x 8 reps
Good Mornings	2 x 8 reps
Standing Calves	2 x 8 reps

AVOIDING THE LOSS OF LEG SPEED

After completing all distance runs, the runner should always finish off the workout with fast strides to help preserve their leg speed:

Do As Follows:

Number of Strides: 4-6 Strides

Distance: 80-100 Meters

Percentage: 80-90%   "Much Faster than the Distance Run"

Surface: Use good flat grass or field turf when ever possible.

BAREFOOT RUNNING: Make sure the grass is safe of debris and run bare foot. This will feel good and strengthen the tendons, ligaments and small muscle groups of the feet. The running shoe acts as a "cast" and does nothing to strengthen the foot.

THE IMPORTANCE OF FLEXIBILITY

Even distance runners need good flexibility to stay injury free. One common injury that I have seen in recent years is a tight IT ban near the outside of the knee. The IT ban is a very hard muscle to stretch, but can be done! I suggest purchasing a *Stretch-Rite Belt*.

This device does the stretching that you normally would have to have a second person help you with. This is a great device that comes with a "color" instruction guide that will show you how to stretch your quads, hips, and the IT ban and many
more body parts.

Go to **SSEproducts.com** and look for the *Stretch-Rite Belt*

HILL TRAINING

Hill training is critical to the success of all track and field athletes. Finding and running hills during the cross country season is a must! Runners that continue to train on hills several days a week even during the track and field season will also benefit! When doing interval training for runners, hills this will also help to make the runner to become stronger & faster.

Hills with a 5% to 10% steepness is all you need in training. While doing downhill running be careful not to over do this. This type of jarring may hurt the lower back, hamstrings knees and hips

USING THE PROPER TRAINING SURFACE

To preserve the young runner, it is critical that they you try to train on different training surface's such as:

1. Grass
2. Wood Chip Running Trails
3. Dirt
4. Cinders
5. Field Turf

These surfaces will help to preserve the runner's body and reduce injuries.

By training of softer surfaces this will actually seem harder, but in the long run will aid the young runner by strengthening the runner's tendon's ligaments and small muscle groups in the foot and ankle. Once this athlete returns to the harder track surface, they will become a stronger and faster athlete. Pounding the concrete might seem faster that training on softer surfaces but it will increase the chance for injuries such as stress fractures
and knee problems.

CALCULATING

WORKOUT

TIMES

How to Calculate the Times for Workouts

All of these cookbooks for training are set up on percentages instead of times.

Due to the fact that your could be training athletes from ages 8 to 18 years old with this book, this method is the most effective way to set up training programs for young athletes.

Also this book will be used by both male and female athletes.

Here are two examples how to calculate the time they should hit for their workouts.

Example #1

Athletes Personal Best Performance for 200 meters: <u>24.0 seconds</u>

80% Effort: <u>30.0 seconds</u>   70% Effort: <u>34.3 seconds</u>

Example #2

Athletes Personal Best Performance for 400 Meters: <u>52.0 seconds</u>

80% Effort: <u>65 seconds</u>   70% Effort: <u>74.3 seconds</u>

Please refer to the percentage charts on the next two pages or do the math to calculate the times they should hit.

Good luck!

Best Time	PERCENTAGE EFFORT					
	95%	90%	85%	80%	75%	70%
1	1.1	1.15	1.2	1.25	1.4	1.45
2	2.1	2.3	2.4	2.5	2.7	2.8
3	3.2	3.4	3.5	3.8	4.0	4.3
4	4.3	4.5	4.7	5.0	5.4	5.8
5	5.3	5.6	5.9	6.3	6.7	7.2
6	6.4	6.7	7.1	7.5	8.0	8.6
7	7.4	7.8	8.3	8.7	9.4	10.0
8	8.5	8.9	9.4	10.0	10.7	11.5
9	9.5	10.0	10.6	11.2	12.0	12.8
10	10.6	11.2	11.8	12.5	13.4	14.3
11	11.6	12.3	13.0	13.8	14.7	15.8
12	12.6	13.4	14.1	15.0	16.0	17.2
13	13.7	14.5	15.3	16.3	17.4	18.6
14	14.8	15.6	16.5	17.5	18.7	20.0
15	15.8	16.7	17.7	18.8	20.0	21.5
16	16.9	17.7	18.9	20.0	21.4	22.9
17	17.9	18.9	20.0	21.3	22.7	24.3
18	19.0	20.0	21.8	22.5	24.0	25.7
19	20.0	21.2	22.4	23.8	25.4	27.2
20	21.1	22.3	23.6	25.0	26.7	28.6
21	22.1	22.3	24.7	26.3	28.0	30.0
22	23.2	24.4	25.9	27.5	29.4	31.5
23	24.3	25.5	27.1	28.8	30.7	32.9
24	25.3	26.7	28.3	30.0	32.0	34.3
25	26.4	27.8	29.5	31.3	33.4	35.8
26	27.4	28.9	30.6	32.5	34.7	37.2
27	28.5	30.0	31.8	33.8	36.0	38.6
28	29.5	31.2	33.0	35.0	37.4	40.0
29	30.6	32.3	32.2	36.3	38.7	41.4
30	31.6	33.3	35.3	37.5	40.0	42.9
31	32.7	34.4	36.5	38.8	41.4	44.3
32	33.7	35.6	37.7	40.0	42.7	45.8
33	34.7	36.7	38.8	41.2	44.0	47.2
34	35.8	37.8	40.0	42.5	45.4	48.6
35	36.9	38.9	41.8	43.8	46.7	50.0

BEST TIME	95%	90%	85%	80%	75%	70%
36	37.9	40.0	42.4	45.0	48.0	51.9
37	38.9	41.2	43.5	46.3	49.4	52.9
38	40.0	42.3	44.8	47.5	50.7	54.3
39	41.1	43.4	45.9	48.8	52.0	55.8
40	42.1	44.5	47.1	50.0	53.4	57.2
41	43.2	45.6	48.3	51.3	54.7	58.6
42	44.2	46.7	49.5	52.5	56.0	60.0
43	45.3	47.8	50.6	53.8	57.8	61.5
44	46.4	48.9	51.8	55.0	58.7	62.9
45	47.4	50.0	53.0	56.3	60.0	64.3
46	48.5	51.1	54.2	57.5	61.4	65.8
47	49.5	52.2	55.3	58.8	62.7	67.2
48	50.6	53.4	56.5	60.0	64.0	68.6
49	51.6	54.5	57.7	61.3	65.4	70.0
50	52.7	55.6	58.9	62.5	66.7	71.5
51	53.7	56.7	60.0	63.8	68.0	72.9
52	54.8	57.8	61.8	65.0	69.4	74.3
53	55.8	58.9	62.4	66.3	70.7	75.8
54	56.9	60.0	63.6	67.5	72.0	77.8
55	57.9	61.2	64.8	68.8	73.4	78.6
56	59.0	62.3	65.9	70.0	74.7	80.0
57	60.0	63.4	67.1	71.2	76.0	81.5
58	61.1	64.5	68.3	72.5	77.3	82.8
59	62.1	65.5	69.4	73.8	78.7	84.3
1:00	63.2	66.7	70.6	75.0	80.0	85.8
1:01	64.2	67.8	71.8	76.3	81.4	87.2
1:02	65.3	68.9	73.0	77.5	82.7	88.6
1:03	66.4	70.0	74.2	78.8	84.0	90.0
1:04	67.4	71.2	75.3	80.0	85.4	91.5
1:05	68.5	72.3	76.5	81.3	86.7	92.9
1:06	69.5	73.3	77.7	82.5	88.0	94.3
1:07	70.6	74.4	78.9	83.4	89.4	95.8
1:08	71.6	75.6	80.0	85.0	90.7	97.7
1:09	72.7	76.7	81.2	86.3	92.0	98.6
1:10	73.7	77.8	82.4	87.5	93.3	99.9

IMPORTANCE OF THE MORNING RUN
&
WEEKEND RUNS

The morning & weekend distance run is critical to the development of the following events:

- **Sprints**
- **Hurdles**
- **400 Meters**
- **800 Meters**

This light distance run if done 2-3 morning a weeks can give the runner extra strength to be successful in their main event. The morning run should be done from 12 to 25 minutes. If you can do this on a soft surface such as grass or cinders, this will help to protect the athlete.

This morning run is also valuable in flushing out lactic acid from the previous day's workout. This morning run is also highly valuable in preparing the athletes for their normal afternoon workout by helping to stimulate and relaxing the muscles. This is of great assistance for preparing the body for a great workout later in the day.

The morning run is also highly valuable for those athletes that are overweight. This additional workout will help the body to "burn" additional calories which over a period of time 3-6 weeks, will aid the athletes to lose weight. Fat weighs more than lean muscle mass. Remember this statement: **"FAT DOES NOT FLY"**

Morning runs are like a *"Savings Account"*, the more money you put in a savings account over a period of 8-12 months, then the more **"MONEY + INTEREST"** you will have at the end of the year. When the important time comes to withdraw your large nest egg, you are ready for your major **"GOAL PURCHASE"**.

Morning Runs can be done before you go to class or when you have a break between classes. If you are going to take a shower anyway get up 25 minutes earlier and go for a light run before you take your shower and then go to class. Only a few athletes will ever have enough **"SELF-DISCIPLINE"** to do morning runs.

Even a smaller group of athletes will ever be a **Conference Champion, State Champion, All-American or NCAA "Individual" National Champion.**   *The choice is yours!*

PACE CHART
(100 to 3,200 Meters)

100	200	300	400	500	600	800	1000	1200	1600	2000	2400	3200
11.00	22.00	33.00	44									
11.25	22.50	33.75	45									
11.50	23.00	34.50	46	57.50								
11.75	23.50	35.25	47	58.75								
12.00	24.00	36.00	48	60.00	01:12.0							
12.25	24.50	36.75	49	01:01.3	01:13.5							
12.50	25.00	37.50	50	01:02.5	01:15.0							
12.75	25.50	38.25	51	01:03.7	01:16.5							
13.00	26.00	39.00	52	01:05.0	01:18.0	1:44						
13.25	26.50	39.75	53	01:06.3	01:19.5	1:46						
13.50	27.00	40.50	54	01:07.5	01:21.0	1:48						
13.75	27.50	41.25	55	01:08.8	01:22.5	1:50	02:17.5					
14.00	28.00	42.00	56	01:10.0	01:24.0	1:52	02:20.0					
14.25	28.50	42.75	57	01:11.3	01:25.5	1:54	02:22.5	2:51				
14.50	29.00	43.50	58	01:12.5	01:27.0	1:56	02:25.0	2:54				
14.75	29.50	44.25	59	01:13.8	01:28.5	1:58	02:27.5	2:57	3:56			
15.00	30.00	45.00	60	01:15.0	01:30.0	2:00	02:30.0	3:00	4:00			
15.25	30.50	45.75	61	01:16.3	01:31.5	2:02	02:32.5	3:03	4:04	5:05		
15.50	31.00	46.50	62	01:17.5	01:33.0	2:04	02:35.0	3:06	4:08	5:10	6:12	
15.75	31.50	47.25	63	01:18.8	01:34.5	2:06	02:37.5	3:09	4:12	5:18	6:15	
16.00	32.00	48.00	64	01:20.0	01:36.0	2:08	02:40.0	3:12	4:16	5:20	6:18	8:32
16.25	32.50	48.75	65	01:21.3	01:37.5	2:10	02:42.5	3:15	4:20	5:25	6:21	8:40
16.50	33.00	49.50	66	01:22.5	01:39.0	2:12	02:45.0	3:18	4:24	5:30	6:24	8:48
16.75	33.50	50.25	67	01:23.8	01:40.5	2:14	02:47.5	3:21	4:28	5:35	6:27	8:56
17.00	34.00	51.00	68	01:25.0	01:42.0	2:16	02:50.0	3:24	4:32	5:40	6:30	9:04
17.25	34.50	51.75	69	01:26.3	01:43.5	2:18	02:52.5	3:27	4:36	5:45	6:33	9:12
17.50	35.00	52.50	70	01:27.5	01:45.0	2:20	02:55.0	3:30	4:40	5:50	6:36	9:20
17.75	35.50	53.25	71	01:28.8	01:46.5	2:22	02:57.5	3:33	4:44	5:55	6:39	9:28
18.00	36.00	54.00	72	01:30.0	01:48.0	2:24	03:00.0	3:36	4:48	6:00	6:42	9:36
18.25	36.50	54.75	73	01:31.3	01:49.5	2:26	03:02.5	3:39	4:52	6:05	6:45	9:44
18.50	37.00	55.50	74	01:32.5	01:51.0	2:28	03:05.0	3:42	4:56	6:10	6:48	9:52
18.75	37.50	56.25	75	01:33.8	01:52.5	2:30	03:07.5	3:45	5:00	6:15	6:51	10:00
19.00	38.00	57.00	76	01:35.0	01:54.0	2:32	03:10.0	3:48	5:04	6:20	6:54	10:08
19.25	38.50	57.75	77	01:36.3	01:55.5	2:34	03:12.5	3:51	5:08	6:25	6:57	10:16
19.50	39.00	58.50	78	01:37.5	01:57.0	2:36	03:15.0	3:54	5:12	6:30	7:00	10:24
19.75	39.50	59.25	79	01:38.8	01:58.5	2:38	03:17.5	3:57	5:16	6:35	7:03	10:32
20.00	40.00	60.00	80	01:40.0	02:00.0	2:40	03:20.0	4:00	5:20	6:40	7:06	10:40
20.25	40.50	60.75	81	01:41.3	02:01.5	2:42	03:22.5	4:03	5:24	6:45	7:09	10:48
20.50	41.00	61.50	82	01:42.5	02:03.0	2:44	03:25.0	4:06	5:28	6:50	7:12	10:56

20.75	41.50	62.25	**83**	01:43.8	02:04.5	**2:46**	03:27.5	4:09	**5:32**	6:55	7:15	11:04
21.00	42.00	63.00	**84**	01:45.0	02:06.0	**2:48**	03:30.0	4:12	**5:36**	7:00	7:18	11:12
21.25	42.50	63.75	**85**	01:46.2	02:07.5	**2:50**	03:32.5	4:15	**5:40**	7:05	7:21	11:20
21.50	43.00	64.50	**86**	01:47.5	02:09.0	**2:52**	03:35.0	4:18	**5:44**	7:10	7:24	11:28
21.75	43.50	65.25	**87**	01:48.8	02:10.5	**2:54**	03:37.5	4:21	**5:48**	7:15	7:27	11:36
22.00	44.00	66.00	**88**	01:50.0	02:12.0	**2:56**	03:40.0	4:24	**5:52**	7:20	7:30	11:44
22.25	44.50	66.75	**89**	01:51.3	02:13.5	**2:58**	03:42.5	4:27	**5:56**	7:25	7:33	11:52
22.50	45.00	67.50	**90**	01:52.5	02:15.0	**3:00**	03:45.0	4:30	**6:00**	7:30	7:36	12:00
22.75	45.50	68.25	**91**	01:53.8	02:16.5	**3:02**	03:47.5	4:33	**6:04**	7:35	7:39	12:08
23.00	46.00	69.00	**92**	01:55.0	02:18.0	**3:04**	03:50.0	4:36	**6:08**	7:40	7:42	12:16

PREPARING

THE

MIND

FOR

SPORTS

POSITIVE MENTAL IMAGERY

In the sport of track and field it is often stated that the sport is 85% mental. This simply means that if an athlete is mentally tough, they will be successful and win many races. You can be a highly trained athlete with great natural ability, but if you are not mentally tough, you are no better off than the average athlete who is an intense competitor. Many world class and college athletes use a sports psychologist to insure that their mental approach to sports is correct!

Speaking success is one way to channel the mental energy of a kid. The next step is to leverage their imagination to achieve a positive outcome.

There is nothing more powerful than a young athlete's imagination. In their minds, there are no limitations. If you will take the time to observe a kid, you will find that he or she could be a professional athlete, Olympian or even the President of the United States. Even if your athletes are older and don't pretend they are superheroes anymore, you can still tap into that powerful sources of belief and imagination to help them improve their athletic performance!

Many kids have a sports hero they admire and want to emulate. So, who are we to stand in their way?   Capturing Imagination is a tool for Success. Using their hero and your kids name in the same sentence is empowering! Leverage their youthful brain power by allowing them to harness their dreams and imagination!

Maybe your athlete thinks they are one of the following track and field stars:

- ➤ Usain Bolt
- ➤ Michael Johnson
- ➤ Galen Rupp
- ➤ Steve Prefontaine
- ➤ Allen Johnson

The term used for imagining a successful outcome before it happens is called imagery. Imagery can be taught to young athletes who have the basic skills to perform the task. Many of you seen "imagery" in motion when watching professional sports athletes.

Some place kickers in football will prepare for making the field goal by mimicking the kick first before they get the ball placed to kick. They are imagining" nothing but net" before they kick the ball. As coaches and parents, it is essential to get young athletes visioning and imagining a positive outcome before it happens.

YOU

ARE

WHAT

YOU

DREAM

ABOUT!

STEPS TO FOCUS ON FUTURE RESULTS

1. Teach the athlete to "see in advance" they are the first out of the starting blocks.

2. Teach the athletes to "lock into the target" with his or her eyes. In most, not all cases, the athlete can be still prior to executing the action (running, hurdling, and jumping). Being steady immediately prior to the action helps with accuracy. He/she needs to see the outcome play in his/her mind's eye for several seconds prior to "initiating the movement". Example: seeing your-self make the first hand-off during the 4 x 100 meter Relay while running the lead-off leg.

3. Teach the player to "see results" verses mechanics. Do not focus on form or technique when executing a skill. A player can have perfect form and still miss the objective. The body will do exactly what the brain tells it to do. If the athlete is thinking about how high his elbow is when hurdling, he or she is not focused on the result.

4. Teach the athletes to "rewind" if the player is unable to remove distractions or worry sets in, have him/her re-wind the video in his or her head, and play it over with the correct results.

Imagery is a very powerful brain tool that can be used by any age. Visualizing a positive result will help athletes gain more focus and control on and off the completion field or track. Remember:

Expect Good Things to Happen and They Will

On the next page is a famous quote by John McDonnell winner of 42 NCAA Championships at the University of Arkansas:

Losing

Is

A

Habit

&

Winning

is a Habit!

GETTING THE MENTAL EDGE

While working with the Zambia Olympic Team at the 1992 Summer Olympic Games in Barcelona, Spain I remember one evening in the Olympic Village which I sat down in the athletic cafeteria for dinner one evening. The person I sat down next to was former University Arkansas & World Class Jumper Michael Conley. Mike was scheduled to compete in the Triple Jump-Final the next evening. During our dinner conversation Mike made one very bold statement to me which was

"I am going to Win the Olympic Triple Jump Competition Tomorrow Evening"

Michael Conley did just that winning with a jump of 59'1" inches which would have been a new world record except the win reading was 2.1 meters per second. This was just over the allowable, as a legal wind reading cannot exceed 2.0 meters per second. Michael Conley's mind was already positive and he could see in his mind that he would become the 1992 Olympic Triple Jump Champion in the next 24 hours.

As a coach who has worked at the high school, junior college and the NCAA university level for almost 30 years, I am a firm believer in the old saying:

You Are What You Say You Are & Believe!

Words are very powerful. They represent what we believe about ourselves. The great inventor Henry Ford was noted for the following quote:

"Whether you believe you can do a thing or not, you are right"

As a coach or parent, you have the ability to teach your kids how to speak and think successful outcomes into reality. Listen to what they say when they make a mistake.

Do you hear things such as?

> ➤ I am terrible at hurdling
> ➤ The other team is better than us
> ➤ I can't take a relay stick
> ➤ It's too hard to run the 400 meters
> ➤ I am never going to be good at track.
> ➤ My legs are too short.

- Trying to run the mile was dumb
- I am not strong enough to throw the shot put
- The 100 meters is too short of an event
- The coach hates me

Young athletes are naturally prone to be self-critical, especially between the ages of 9-14. They are naturally critical of others.

The coach must be positive at all times. Teach your athletes to be positive and to select their words correctly!

You must remember the golden rule:

POSITIVE

THOUGHTS

BRING

POSITIVE

RESULTS

99%
Concentration
Equals
100%
Failure

METHODS TO INCREASE POSITIVE SELF TALK

1. Many parents allow critical and negative statements made by their children to go unnoticed. Most of the time the parent makes similar negative and critical statements, modeling an unproductive attitude. Avoid negativity and criticism yourself, and when you hear critical statements from your child, firmly and kindly ash them to turn the statement into a positive statement.

2. Keep the young athlete focused on what he or she can do. Remind athletes of examples of their success.

3. Guild the young athlete into speaking encouraging positive words to others on the team and even their opponents! Many adults need to learn this. Encouraging, positive words keeps your children, teammates and opponents focused on good play.

4. Be an example: Always speak well of your efforts and others' efforts. Watch your own talk where you may have a tendency to beat yourself up or belittle others. It is simply wrong and creates a negative, non-productive environment.

Young athletes are much more likely to respond to tough love and not demeaning criticism. Perhaps being a positive communicator is not easy since many of us have grown up with a military style of leadership on the playing field focused on barking out orders, chastising or whipping us into shape.

There are many great motivation movies because they typify overcoming the great odds and coming out a winner.

Such Positive Motivational Movies are as follows:

- ➢ Rocky

- ➢ Coach Carter

- ➢ Chariots of Fire

- ➢ Remember the Titians

- ➢ Pre

If coaches are attempting to speak success into the lives of the young athletes they must also follow the golden rule Say things you would want someone else to say to you! That will make you think twice about calling the referee or the starter a dummy or a four letter word.

Also Body language is critical. Even though you might not say a word, a certain look or gesture can say more than words. Coaches can say a lot without a word.

They say it takes nine positive statements to undo one negative one. Keep your feedback positive, and your athletes will shine and perform to the best of their ability.

If you must correct an athlete, a good mental picture to help you remember is to think of feedback as a sandwich. As a sandwich-two "positives", one at the beginning and one at the end, with the "corrective information" in the middle of your statement.

In summary teaching young athletes to say positive things about themselves and others will ensure they will grow up to be encouragers themselves.

85%

Of

Track & Field

Is

Mental!

Visualize & Dream Success

Day's/Minutes/Seconds

Before

Your

Competition!

MENTAL PREPERATION FOR SPORTS
By
Coach Steve Silvey

It is important that you increase the athletes focus and commitment to sports with goal setting. Once parents and coaches get on the same page and understand each other's goals and motives, the next step is to talk with your young athlete about the following:

> What do you want to accomplish in the sport?

> Is your athlete ready to work towards their team goals?

> What is your athlete is hoping to improve or learn from this sport?

Many young athletes are involved in sports due to their parent's desire. The athlete participates hoping to please the parent. Still the young athlete needs to have his/her own goals! The young athlete should have goals beyond trying to please their coach. Often, coaches just assume their athletes will get in line with their coaches' goals. If this doesn't happen, coaches can easily become frustrated with athletes who don't share their adult goals. Remember:

Every Kid Needs His or Her Personal Goal for Sports

Children are natural goal setters, but too often those goals are not articulated or even discussed. Goal setting teaches responsibility and focus at any age.

NEVER tell a young athlete that he or she can't do something athletically! One exercise you should do with your athletes is to announce at the next practice that you want them to come with one goal.

That goal should pertain to a specific activity in their sport like one of the following:

> Running faster time

> Winning a Game

> Betting a Rival Team

> Setting a School Record

That goal is to a great extent the outcome of individual work each player puts into his/her personal goals.

A great way to set goals is using the **"SMART"** principal

Specific-Focus on a specific skill that will help him/her contributes to winning. Example: is timing a child's 50 meter dash as this shows they are more fit.

Measureable-Good goal setting includes a way to measure whether the goal was met or not. Example: broke 10 seconds for the 60 meter dash

Achieve-Means the goal is within the reach of the athlete. Example: A goal that can be accomplished with in the current or upcoming season such as being undefeated in the 40 yard dash!

Realistic-Achievable and Realistic go hand in hand. This is a balancing act. To be in your first year as a track athlete and to say I am going to break the National High School Record is not being realistic.

Timely-Placing a time frame on your children's goal is very important; otherwise the goal will become less meaningful. If the time frame is ignored, it sets the athlete up for learning to procrastinate. This is a habit that can easily extend into adulthood. Example: I will break the 9th grade school record this season for the 1 mile run.

SMART GOALS EXERCISES

1. On two (2) Index cards, write down their goals. One is for the coach and one is for the athlete. The goal should be the same on both cards

2. Have the student place their goal card in a location in their home that they will see every day. Such as mirror, closet door, bulletin board or the refrigerator.

3. Before each practice, ask your athletes to remember their goals and ask them to practice hard with their goals in the mind.

SMART GOAL

This season I am going to:

_____

I am going to achieve this how many times:

_____

I will achieve my goals by doing the following things each practice:

1._____

2._____

3._____

4._____

I know I can reach my goal because: _____

_____

I will complete my goal by: DATE: _____

MANAGING STRESS IN KEY COMPETITIONS

The effects of stress, whether it creates anticipation or anxiety, are rooted in how we interpret events. Our brains are programed for survival. The stress response is valuable if our lives or the lives of our loved ones are being threatened. Stress puts bodily functions in motion to create a fight or flight response.

Having some stress in our lives is good. It creates action and a reason to get moving in the morning. Many of us perform well when we have optimal amounts of stress. However, performance is affected when we reach or exceed our stress threshold.

Feeling of anxiety, worry, and fear begin to take over which are emotions that are always a negative for sports.

Some of the Major Causes of Stress in Young Athletes:

➢ Too Much Hype for the Sporting Event They Are Competing In

➢ Practice Doesn't Allow for Free play & Fun

➢ Doing Too Many Activities

➢ Pressure of Letting Down His or Her Team Members

➢ Being Asked to Compete at a Higher level that they Are Capable

➢ Fear of losing Esteem with Parents

As a coach, you may help calm the athlete down and help them get re-focused using the following methods:

✓ Allow the Athlete to Cry

✓ Allow the Athlete To Vent

✓ Teach The Athlete To Take A Deep Breath

✓ Remind the Athlete They Are Capable of Getting the Job done on the Athletic Field

✓ Offer The athlete Specific Feedback That will Help Them Reach Their Goal Next Time

✓ Lead By Example: Be A Positive & Upbeat

✓ Be a Good Role Model For Your Athletes

Emotional outburst by your young athletes is obvious indicators that something is wrong with the young athlete. As a coach you must step in quickly by following the above mentioned guideline, and you will teach athletes how to control their emotions and channel their energy into renewed determination

Remember With Regards to Confidence:

Young athletes are able to manage stress and put their performance in perspective. Parents and coaches should be their sounding board for confidence!

REWARDS THAT BUILD THE ATHLETES MENTAL TOUGHNESS

With all the medals, trophies, relay batons and t-shirts and the "way to go" bombarding coaches and players, how do you know when to
provide a reward and what type to provide the athlete with the most motivation?

According to sports psychology research, there are two types of rewards:

EXTRINSIC REWARDS-trophies, medals, cheering, pats on the back and talking to the newspaper, TV or Radio the reporter.

If the player is externally oriented and the extrinsic reward decreases or stops altogether, the athlete may become disillusioned and stop practicing hard. When things don't go their way, extrinsic athletes may suddenly quit or exhibit noticeable dissatisfaction in public or private settings.

INTRINSIC REWARDS- These rewards are what athletes give themselves such as a healthy feeling of satisfaction and pride in their recent performance. This internal feeling of excitement will motivate further achievement regards of the external reward system. Good coaches and parents should work on enforcing intrinsic rewards.

Paying for performance decreases a young athlete's natural motivation to perform. It creates an "entitlement mentality" that our society does not need!

The advantage if Intrinsic Rewards is that you can greatly enhance the mental toughness and positive attitude for competing in sports by focusing on creating intrinsically motivated player

SEVERAL WAYS TO BUILD MOTIVATED ATHLETES

✓ Verbally Praise Goal Achievement with Specific Verbal Rewards

✓ Have all athletes set a single "Individual" goals

✓ The Athlete should set "Team" goals

✓ Have the athletes set realist goals

✓ Get Rid of All "Payment for Performance" Rewards

While coaching at the University of Arkansas from 1994 to 2000, I was part of something very special as our team won 17 out of 18 SEC "Team" Championships and 13 NCAA National "Team" Championships. Each time our Team won the competition our athletes did the famous University of Arkansas chant "Calling the Hogs" which normally always irritated the opposing schools but brought great team pride and unity to our University of Arkansas Track & Field team. We could only do this after winning a major championship.

In Summary, remember that young athletes are natural achievers that don't need payment to play! Self-motivated athletes play for personal accomplishment and don't feel entitle to receive accolades for natural talent or just for showing up.

SPECIALATION IN SPORTS

Research shows that there are some benefits to early specialization in sports. Some sports like gymnastics or figure skating need it while there are negative effects to early specialization such as:

Limits to Motor Skill Development- Motor skill development occurs when young athletes are exposed to a variety of physical challenges. It isn't good for young athletes to be limited in this area of motor skill development.

Loss of Fun Factor-Practices focused on a repetitive skill, requires a young athlete to focus on the task instead of building rapport with other team members. This causes them to lose out in socializing with other kids. This play becomes work and no kid likes work!

Overuse Injury- Repetitive drills at an early age, without adequate rest and recovery, places tremendous stress on growing bones and joints. If you are choosing early specialization and repetitive drills for your child, please tell his or her pediatrician so that he/she can educate you about the health risks involved.

There is no present evidence to support the notion that early specialization and repetitive training are the keys to success in sports later in like. Giving young athletes a diverse experience in physical activities, including sports, is the best rule to follow.

You will find that many elite athletes today had a very diverse sports background when growing up versus a specialized background. Learning the strategies of different sports and developing the skills for different sports made the athletes more well-rounded and more equipment to handle the demands of the sport they choose. Let young athletes play a variety of sports while they are still young. By the time they hit adolescence, they will specialize on their own. The scholarships and professional sports options will come to those young players who are talents enough and who are not burned out by that time. Remember:

EARLY DIVERSIFICATION
&
NOT SPECIALIZATION IS THE KEY!

DAY

OF

THE

TRACK

MEET

TRACK MEET-"WARM-UP" Routine

2 hours before your event: See the trainer for Treatment or Taping

1 hour 35 Minutes prior to your event: Light Jogging 1,200 to 1,600 meters

1 hour 15 minutes before your event: Stretch-Rite Belt OR Static Stretching
(15-20 minutes)

55 Minutes Before your event: Dynamic flexibility Drills (8 each leg)
leg swings, side to side leg swings, hip circles. bicycles, inverted scissors, sagital scissors, single leg donkey kicks, hurdle seat leg pick-ups, hurdle seat exchanges, eagles, stomach eagles, Lung exchanges & lung walks.

45 Minutes Before your event: Hurdle-Rhythm Drills

35 Minutes Before your event: Sprint Drills-Do 8 (including fast legs & butt kicks)

30 Minutes Before your event: Hurdlers: 5 x5 lead/Trail leg Drills

25 Minutes Before your event: 5 x 60 Meter Stride Build-ups (PROGRESSION)
1st Stride= 60%
2nd Stride=70%
3rd Stride= 80%
4th Stride= 90%
5th Stride= 95%   "RACE EFFORT"

DO YOUR FINAL RACE CHECK-IN & GET YOUR RACE HIP NUMBER!

20 Minutes Before your event: SPRINTERS: 4-5 20 meter block starts (90-95%)
HURDLERS: 3 x 1 Hurdle x 2 x 2 hurdles(90-95%)

YOUR FAST-TWITCH MUSCLE FIBERS SHOULD BE STIMULATED 100%

15 minutes before your event: Relax!
Stretch
Elevate Feet for 5 minutes against a wall
Visualize Success in your Mind (Your Perfect Race)

2-3 Minutes before your race: Adjust starting blocks
Do 1-2 (Jump Tucks) in air for "Explosiveness"
Take 1-2 Deep Breathes while in starting blocks

GUN   React Quickly to the "SOUND" of the GUN!
Explode from blocks pushing with legs & driving hard with your ARMS!

HOW TO PERFORM AT 100% of YOUR TRACK ABILITY
By
Coach Steve Silvey
Sprints/Hurdles/Relays
Texas Tech University

Do YOU understand how to get 100% + from your body? Here are a few tips to help you.

1. Hydrating properly means using the restroom a minimum of every 45 minutes to an hour, then you not hydrated properly. (100+ oz. of fluids every day accomplishes this).

2. Don't let cool weather fool you! Even on cool days it is important to drink 100 ounces of fluid a day.

3. On the day of the meet stay away from fried or greasy foods and the following meats such as: ANY FORM OF BEEF, Bacon, Sausage, etc.

4. Bananas ARE your friend and a MUST for everyday. Each morning eat 1-2 bananas. Potassium is found in bananas. It is a mineral that assists in muscle contraction and in maintaining fluid and electrolyte balance in body cells. Potassium is also important in sending nerve impulses as well as releasing energy from protein, fat, and carbohydrates during metabolism. If you can't eat bananas then it is VITAL that you take some **Phosphate Plus tablets**. This helps your muscles to stay loose & limber!   Phosphate Plus can be found at this website: *SSEproducts.com*

5. You need electrolytes in the body. Electrolytes are important because they are what your cells (especially nerve, heart, muscle) use to maintain voltages across their cell membranes and to carry electrical impulses (nerve impulses, muscle contractions) across themselves and to other cells. Your kidneys work to keep the electrolyte concentrations in your blood constant despite changes in your body. For example, when you exercise heavily, you lose electrolytes in your sweat, particularly sodium and potassium. These electrolytes must be replaced to keep the electrolyte concentrations of your body fluids constant. So, many sports drinks have sodium chloride or potassium chloride added to them. They also have sugar and flavorings to provide your body with extra energy and to make the drink taste better. So drink 1/2 bottle of **"Pedalyte"**1-2 hours prior to your race and 1/2 of the bottle prior to your second event.

6. A great warm-up is the key! Too many athletes do a very poor job and end of running a sub-par race because your engine was never properly warmed-up. Start your warm-up 1 hour prior to your event.

7. Always do 5 stride build-ups of 60 meters, 15-20 minutes prior to your event. Progression for the stride build-ups should be as follows (60%,70%,80%,90%, 95%). **The last stride should be as fast as anything in your race!**

8. In cool weather, add an additional 15-20 minutes to your warm-up time. In other words instead of starting 1 hour prior, you start 1 hour 15-20 minutes prior.

9. In cool weather wear spandex half-tights and/or a spandex top under your jersey. Only use long tights in practice.

10. How do you know if you have "warmed up" properly…by your sweat! If you have done a proper "warm-up", you will be sweating prior to the EVEN in cool weather!

- 1200 meters of Jogging
- 20 minutes of Static Stretching or 20 minute of Stretch-Rite Belt
- Dynamic Flexibility Drills
- Hurdle/Rhythm Drills (Side Skips, Walk-Overs, Over-Unders, A, B and C, skips)
- Sprint Drills (6-8 Drills of your choice)
- 5 x 60 meter Stride Build-ups (60%,70%,80%, 90%,95%)
- "Positive" Mental Imagery Prior to the Race – wipe everyone and everything from your mind. Now visualize your best time or best race – how did it feel at the start, over each hurdle or around each curve? When did you "kick in?" What did that feel like? What did it feel like when you crossed the finish? Now visualize it again! Be ready to FOCUS and have fun running the best you have ever run!

CHECKOUT: SSEproducts.com

For more Track and Field Products

Be the Champion You Want To Be

Be a Goal Setter - Understand the goals must be pushed by <u>passion</u>. If your goals do not make you feel sick to think about missing them, give you the strength and courage you need to do what you need to do to achieve them, and motivate you when you think about them, something very important is missing.

Be Here - Never miss a practice or a meeting. You all made the smart decision to be part of this team! There is always something to learn and gain everyday whether at practice or at a team meeting. Everyone needs to be re-focused and re-energized and where does that happen? At practice and with your team!

Be Positive – Your POSITIVE ATTITUDE is the most important things you can have. *You are in control of your attitude.* Who you are around, what you read, what you listen to and the words you choose to say all determine your attitude. *Never talk about other people and never talk negatively about yourself.*

Be a "TEAM" Player - Create your circle of influence. Take advice only from people you are willing to trade places with. Team up with people who are willing to work as hard as you are. Stay in the space of people who have a vision for what is possible with the Track & Field Team. Run from people who do not have a dream or a goal. They may try to steal yours or take you down with them.

Become a Skills Master - Master the skills of your event. Mastering the fundamental skills is critical. When the adrenalin and excitement takes over the skills you have mastered will be what carries you to success.

Become a Master of Your Emotion - Emotional management. You will have disappointments – Big disappointments. Life challenges. You are not alone. People will disappoint you and you will disappoint yourself. The character within will determine how you face your life disappointments today and in your future. Every one has things happen to them – the way you choose to deal with them is what makes you a champion or not.

Become a Time Manager- as leaders you must manage your time. We all have the same number of minutes and hours in a day. What we do with it is the difference between those who become champions and those who don't. You're most important "team" time is doing what you need to do to stay academically on track and get your degree. You're most important Track & Field time is spent on the track and in the weight room.

Developing Your Skills. Your most important personal time is being with those who support your goals, help you relax and don't encourage activities or thoughts that affect you negatively. Time is the one commodity you can't get back - use your time wisely.

Be Organized – If necessary make a "To Do" list Daily. Stay focused and on track with the things you are suppose to do, not just what you feel like doing. Good days, turn into good weeks that turn into good months that turn out champions.

Be Focused - In your academic and athletic life focus on the activity not results. Of course the results are important but more important are the activity that leads to the wanted results. Do your workouts – they never disappoint you. Understand what you must do daily, weekly and monthly to have the results you want.

Be Aware of Your Image – inside and out. Are you looking, acting, and being a good example of athletic excellence? Others are watching you – what you do and what you say. As a athlete be committed to excellence. Your commitment inspires others. Your high standard of excellence automatically moves your team in the direction of excellence. Excellence starts with image which includes how you treat others on and off of the track.

Be Enthusiastic in Al You do. Work with enthusiasm. There is quiet enthusiasm and loud enthusiasm. Both are correct – just make sure you have it and show it. Enthusiasm is contagious – share your's with others.

Be a Team Builder - Build others. Build their skills, build their vision, build their belief, build their understanding of what this team stands for and build their responsibility to excellence. Leadership is a very important position. Do not take it lightly.

Be Grateful and Appreciative - Appreciate and have gratitude. Gratitude is critical. Are you honestly grateful for what you have? Are you honestly grateful for where you are? Are you honestly grateful that you have this opportunity to work hard? Think of your friends from high school who would love to have this opportunity and when you're tired and feel like you can't run another step or lift another weight, remember this gift you have been given, find your positivity and look forward to the great future you have ahead because you did run another step and you did lift that extra weight and you are going the extra mile.

PART-TIME ATHLETES GET PART-TIME RESULTS

SUPER-NUTRITION FOR TRACK & FIELD

SUPER-NUTRITION

Stay away from these so called energy drinks such as Red Bull and Monster Drinks they contain extremely high levels of caffeine or illegal supplements. These can lead to dehydration or produce a very high heart rate that could lead to death!

From a track and field standpoint, there is an illegal drug list of more than 150 banned substances. If an athlete takes one by mistake, they could be banned for a period of 1-4 years by the NCAA or the U.S.A. Olympic Committee or other governing associations.

Many of these suspensions happen because athletes will walk into a sports nutrition store in the mall and are told to buy several products that have banned substances in them. So be careful and read the labels!

Stay away from steroids and human growth hormones. These might build muscle mass quick, but now you will be subject to a suspension of 1-4 years by governing sports federations!

It is not worth taking illegal performance drugs just to win a medal as many of the Great Russian and East German Olympic Champions of the 1970's and 1980's are not even alive today. Steroids and Human Growth Hormones will shorten a person's life span by 20-30 years!

With regards to "legal" supplements, I have seen some amazing developments in the training and performance of my athletes since I have begun using some of these in the early 1990's to close the gap on the "Druggies".

According to the Great Olympic 400 Meter Champion and former World Record Holder Lee Evans (43.86) "You can get with 5% of the Drug cheaters with proper nutritional supplements"

I am a firm believer in "legal" nutritional supplements to aid the athlete in their quest to maximize their athletic abilities.

Some of these items are as follows:

1. Multiple Vitamins

2. Phosphate Supplement

3. Calcium/Magnesium Supplement (Osteo-Tech)

4. Fruit/Vegetable Supplement

5. Protein Supplement (Creatine)

6. Vitamin D-3

I have been using **Phosphates (*Phosphate Plus*)** with my athletes for almost 20 years. They help in reducing muscle cramps, strains, pulls and lactic acid build-up from intense workouts. This is the equivalent to eating 8-9 bananas a day!

I also suggest a calcium/magnesium supplement **(*Osteo-Tech*)** help's the athletes with natural muscle contraction, reduces stress fractures and aids in speeding up athletic injuries such as hamstring strains or pulls. Pure calcium does not get 100% absorption that is why it must be with magnesium!

A fruit and vegetable supplement *(**Fruit & Veggie Power**)* can insure the athlete's gets enough fruits and vegetables in their daily diet.

As long as the young athlete does a great job of consuming 8-10 glasses of water a day, creatine *(**C-Power Sports Creatine**)* is still a great product to help them improve strength levels in young athletes that needs to get stronger. This is like eating 8-10 pounds of red meat a day. No one would want to or be able to afford it!

With regards to *(**Vitamin D-3**)* please go to the top left side of my website **SSEproducts.com** to read an awesome 10 page research article written by a leading medical researcher. Vitamin D-3 is often referred to as the sunshine vitamin. This product is helpful to the athlete in some many positive ways!   So be careful and read the labels!

For further information about these products go to my website:
SSEproducts.com

TRYPTOPHAN
"Strength Builder"

Where Do I Get It?   **Eating Turkey or Tuna**

When: **After 9:00pm prior to going to bed**

Benefits: Natural strength builder & promotes a Better "Deep" sleep!

What is It? L-Trytophan is an essential amino acid and a metabolic precursor to serotonin. Serotonin acts as a chemical messenger or neurotransmitter in the central nervous system and appears to affect the sleep/wake arousal. Serotonin levels in the brain can be increased by the ingestion of L-Tryptophan, and this has been shown to hasten the onset of sleep in humans.

IMPORTANT INFORMATION: As you know, protein's amino acids such as **L-Trytophan** is an essential build block for strengthening and maintaining muscle, repairing damaged tissues and boosting YOUR energy levels!

"GET THE EDGE ON YOU COMPETITION"

Sports Nutrition

If you are a runner, bodybuilder or athlete of any kind, you need to know the benefits of making tuna a regular part of your training diet.

Tuna is one of nature's best sources of high-quality protein.

As you know, protein's amino acids are an essential building block for strengthening and maintaining muscles, repairing damaged tissues and boosting energy levels.

Unlike carbohydrates, which cause an insulin spike that soon leaves you tired and hungry, protein stabilizes blood sugar levels, keeping your appetite in check and your energy levels high.

Plus, tuna and related high protein foods are very low in fat, meaning that you can snack on a can of tuna throughout the day without having to worry about adding excess pounds.

As the date of the athletic contest nears, the low-sodium varieties of tuna become even more critical, giving your body the energy you need without the water-retaining sodium found in many foods.

Whether you eat it plain, on a sandwich, with crackers or as part of low-fat salad, tuna is one of the fastest, most nutritious athletic supplements you can find!

HOW DO I TRIM THE FAT TO RUN FAST?

Why can't I run fast anymore? Why can't I win?

ANSWER: How much do you weigh? Let me ask you a simple question - if I gave you a backpack with 10 pounds of rocks in it, would you run faster wearing the backpack or not wearing it? Not wearing the backpack, of course. I challenge you to try it. Put your books in a backpack and then weigh it. Now go for a short run. What did you feel?

Putting on 4, 5 or 10 pounds gradually doesn't Impact you as dramatically as if you strapped on the 10 pound backpack but the EFFECT on your ability to RUN FAST is exactly the same. What was your weight on the day of your BEST performance? What is it today? If you weigh more, even 4-5 pounds, what makes you think you can perform at your best? How many FAT elite track athletes have you seen at the Olympics or World Championships?

Sprinters who want to perform at a high level should be eating a protein diet supplemented with the right amount of carbs. *Power-to-weight ratio is imperative for sprinters,* therefore *maximizing muscle mass and maintaining low body fat levels* is essential to reaching your full potential.

To lose the fat there are two things that must happen. First you must eat less calories than you burn. In other words eating 5,000 calories a day and burning 3.500 a day equals weight gain.

Eat 3,500 calories a day and burn off 4,000 calories equals weight loss. Once the weight is lost you can go into maintenance mode. That would probably mean increasing your caloric intake to 4,000 per day so that the number of calories burned is close or equal to the number of calories you are eating. Second to lose fat and build muscle you must develop the self-discipline to make smart food choices throughout the day - everyday.

Getting Started:

Morning: Add activity to your daily routine
- Ride an exercise bike or jog for 20 minutes 3-4 days a week.
- Walk (move quickly) to and from class whenever possible. *Don't ride the bus.*
- Exercise on Sunday (as your workout prescribes)
- Walk around the mall at a brisk pace for at least an hour.

Limit your fat intake to 6 - 15 grams per meal - 18 - 30 grams per day of fat
Eat Wisely - first and foremost drink water - 8 oz an hour is a good goal

1. **Large Breakfast** - Limit the carbs
   a. Eat eggs, breakfast meats and wheat toast (if you have to have toast) & only sugar-free jelly
   b. Skim or 1-2% milk
   c. Sugar-free cereals - oatmeal, whole bran, Special K- no Captain Crunch, no Tony the Tiger, or Cocoa Puffs - if you use sweetner try to use Splenda (yellow packet)
   d. No donuts, muffins, bagels and no jellies, no sweet rolls or fruit as it will cause a large insulin jolt and make you want more - if you must have fruit the best choice is an apple

2. **Light Lunch** - *include any of all of the following:*
   a. Any whole-grain bread including whole-grain wheat bread
   b. turkey, tuna, or chicken
   c. Lettuce, tomato
   d. Any hard cheese - cheddar, swiss, etc.
   e. Mustard or low fat mayo
   f. Salad with blue cheese dressing or olive oil and vinegar with spices
   g. Broth-based soups - no creamy soups while trying to lose weight because they are loaded with fat
   h. Fresh fruit - no canned fruit since it often contains white sugar
   i. Fresh vegetables
   j. Substitute olive oil on vegetables for other fats such as butler or margarine
   . k. All-natural Peanut Butter only - other peanut butters contain sugar & unhealthy fat
   l. Skim or 1-2% milk

Do not include:
   a. Cookies, pastries, candy or ice cream of any kind
   b. White bread or any processed foods including white sugar
   c. Creamy soups
   d. Most salad dressings - Ranch, Thousand Island, French, Honey Mustard
   e. Catsup

3. **Good Size** *Dinner that includes:*
   a. Pizza with whole wheal or thin crust - you may want to ask that they go light on the cheese and be careful of the toppings you choose.
   b. Whole wheat pasta (whenever possible) with tomato sauce, vegetables like spinach, broccoli, and chicken or fish - no cream or butter sauces
   c. Grilled or broiled meat- fish, chicken, beef (limited to once a week)
   d. Vegetables fresh or cooked - use olive oil instead of butter
   e. Fresh fruit
   f. Limited bread and only a whole grain bread
   g. Skim or 1-2% milk

OTHER:
   a. 2-3 hours prior to a sustained 90 minute or less workout try eating low-fat yogurt, oatmeal or other low-glycemic carbs.
   b. Eat small amounts (11 or so) almonds or cashews as a snack between meals
   c. Energy bars can have 170 to 300 calories so consider it a "fat food"
   d. No snacking after Dinner (No 10:00pm Pizza's)

Do's
1. Drink plenty of water prior 10 your meal to increase metabolism and make exercise more effective, make you feel full and decrease your appetite
2. Reach for a soda or sport drink, grab water instead
3. Eat large portions of fruits and vegetables at breakfast. lunch & dinner.
4. 48 *hours before a track meet eat fish or chicken* as they digest quicker.
5. Use ground turkey instead of ground hamburger In your cooking.
6. If you must have a steak eat it early in the week (It take 48 hours to digest)

7. Whenever possible eat the fruit instead of drinking the Juice but if you are drinking a fruit juice choose (unsweetened if available) apple juice or apple cider
8. For a late night snack: Orange, Apple or Banana or low fat sugar-free yogurt - limit the bananas to no more than 1 a day until you have reached a maintenance weight. They are loaded with sugar and very little fiber.
9. Eat Fish - and lots of it - but bake it or broil it DO NOT FRY ITI
9. Eat Chicken: Remove the skin and bake it or broil ill
10. East only Whole GRAIN Wheat or Multi-grain breads.
11. Purchase or choose Wheat Pasta when possible. (Most nutritional value)
12. Drink skim or low-fat milk and or eat low fat yogurt.

Don'ts

1. NO Fast Food including Big Mac's and Whopper's (35 to 37 grams of fat)
2. NO Taco Bell (lots of cheap food that is high in calories and fat)
3. NO French fries (ton's of grease & fat)
4. NO Deep Fried foods (Lois of Grease and Fat)
5. NO soft drinks that are sweetened with sugar - If you must have a soft drink, drink Diet Pepsi, Diet Dr. Pepper, Diet Root Beer, Diet Sprite or Diet coke
6. Don't eat Pizza more than once a week. (large amount of calories and fat)
7. Eat Pasta only once or twice a week.
8. Stay away from white foods including white breads and buns. While foods are processed foods, such as sugar and flour. They contain virtually no nutrition and they turn to sugar which is stored as FAT - includes white bread and white pasta -Wheat is a better choice and usually available
9. Limit the number and quantity sports drinks in your diet-they contain mega amounts of sugar which is turned into FAT
10. NO beer and liquor - While training keep in mind that while it may be hard to resist a beer when you are hot and sweaty the sugar in the beer has a higher glycemic index than white bread. The maltose in beer is digested very rapidly which causes large swings in the blood sugar and insulin levels. This insulin response leads to the fat storage in the abdomen that is known as the "beer belly." If you HAVE to have a beer, do it during maintenance and choose a lite one...only one.

Beer and liquor is not the chosen drink of CHAMPIONS!

FAST FOOD CHART

FAST FOOD	AMOUNT	FAT-Grams	CALORIES
Cheeseburger	large	34g	610
Cheeseburger	Regular	15g	320
Hamburger	Large	27g	520
Hamburger	Regular	12g	275
Fish-Battered/Fried	1serving	11g	210
Chicken-Fried-Dark Meat	2 pieces	30g	430
Chicken-Fried- Wing/Breast	2 pieces	30g	495
Chicken Nuggets, Plain	6	18g	300
Sausage, Fried/Battered	1	8g	100
Onion Rings	8	16g	175
Fries	Large	20g	360
Fries	Regular	12g	240
Hash Browns	1/2 cup	9g	150
Corn Dog	1	19g	460
Hot Dog	Regular	15g	240
Hot Dog with Chili	1	18g	325
Dressing-Caesar	1 packet	14g	160
Dressing- French	1 packet	8g	160
Dressing -Ranch	1 packet	21g	230
Pancakes, Butter & Syrup	3	14g	520
Pizza, Cheese	12 inch	20g	900
Pizza, Pepperoni	12 inch	42g	1100
Mex. Burrito, Bean &Meat	2	18g	510
Mex. Burrito Bean	2	15g	450
Mex. Chimichanga, Beef &-Cheese	1	24g	445
Mex. Chimichanga, Beef	1	20g	425
Mex. Enchilada, Cheese & Beef	1	18g	325
Mex. Enchilada, Cheese/S. Cream	1	20g	320
Mex. Nachos, Cheese	8	20g	345
Mex. Taco	Large	32g	550
Mex. Taco	Small	21g	370
Mex. Tostado, Bean & Cheese	1	10g	225

GENERAL

CONDITIONING

PHASE

GENERAL CONDITIONING-Week #1
SPRINTS/ HURDLES/RELAYS

Monday   TEAM MEETING

Tuesday   Jog 800 to 1,200 Meters
Static Stretch/Dynamic Flex/Hurdle Drills/Sprint Drills/5 x 70
Cross Country Run of 2 miles
Med Ball Circuit "Little Dude"

Wednesday   Jog 800 to 1,200 Meters
Static Stretch/Dynamic Flex/Hurdle Drills/Sprint Drills/5 x 70 m
6 x 200 Meters (75%) Grass
Shot Throws X 5
Body Weight Circuit
Cool Down

Thursday   Jog 800 to 1,200 Meters
Static Stretch/Dynamic Flex/Hurdle Drills/Sprint Drills/5 x 70 m
Everyone: 5 x 200 meters Grass (80%)
Plyometrics: 5 x 5 Double Leg Hurdle Hops (Sand)
Cool Down
Weight Room

Friday   Jog 800 to 1,200 Meters
Static Stretch/Dynamic Flex/Hurdle Drills/Sprint Drills/5 x 70
12 x100's (75%) "GRASS"
5 x Resistance Towing
Shot Throws "Bomb"
Body Weight Circuits
Cool Down

Saturday   Rest or 10 minute jog and 6 x 100 strides

Sunday   Active Rest: 2 hours of Basketball, Volleyball, Tennis or soccer

Everyone-Do 2-3 morning runs of 15-20 minutes-EASY*

GENERAL CONDITIONING-Week #2
Sprints/Hurdles/Relays

Monday
Jog 800 to 1,200 Meters
Static Stretch/Dynamic Flex/Hurdle Drills/Sprint Drills/5 x 70
20 minute Cross Country Run 6 x 100 strides on "Grass"
Plyometrics "Plyo-Jam"
Med Ball Circuit "Big Mamma"
Cool Down

Tuesday
Jog 800 to 1,200 Meters
Static Stretch/Dynamic Flex/Hurdle Drills/Sprint Drills/5 x 70 m
SPRINTS: 6 x 200 Meters (75%-80%)   GRASS
400 METERS: 8 x 200 Meters (75-80%) GRASS
Cool Down
Weight Room

Wednesday Jog 800 to 1,200 Meters
Static Stretch/Dynamic Flex/Hurdle Drills/Sprint Drills/5 x 70 me
Plyometrics "Big Sandy"
Shot Throws "Bomb"

Thursday
Jog 800 to 1,200 Meters
Static Stretch/Dynamic Flex/Hurdle Drills/Sprint Drills/5 x 70 m
18 Minute Cross Country Run followed by 5 x 100's Grass
Weight Room

Friday
Jog 800 to 1,200 Meters
Static Stretch/Dynamic Flex/Hurdle Drills/Sprint Drills/5 x 70 m
Running Harness x 5
SPRINTS: 4 x 300 Meters (80%)   GRASS
400 METERS: 6 x 300 Meters (80%) GRASS
Body Weight Circuit
Cool Down

Saturday
12 minute Jog and 8 x 100 meters

Sunday
1 hour of Active Rest Play basketball, Soccer, Tennis or walk

Everyone-Do 2-3 morning runs of 15-20 minutes-EASY***

General Conditioning Training-Week #3
Sprints/Hurdles/Relays

Monday
Jog 800 to 1,200 Meters
Static Stretch/Dynamic Flex/Hurdle Drills/Sprint Drills/5 x 70 m
Plyometrics "Big Sandy"
Sprinters/Hurdlers: 5 x 300 Meters (80%) 4mR   "GRASS"
400 Meters: 7 x 300 Meters (80%) 4mR   "GRASS"
Med Ball Circuit "Big Mamma"
Cool Down

Tuesday
Jog 800 to 1,200 Meters
Static Stretch/Dynamic Flex/Hurdle Drills/Sprint Drills/5 x 70 m
Sprinters: 18 Minute Cross Country Run "GRASS"
400 Meter: 24 Minute Cross Country Run "GRASS"
5 x 100"s GRASS
Cool Down
Weight Room

Wednesday
Jog 800 to 1,200 Meters
Static Stretch/Dynamic Flex/Hurdle Drills/Sprint Drills/5 x 70
Shot Throws "GUN"
15 minute Run   12 x 100's "GRASS"   (75%)
Plyometrics"6 x 5 Double Leg Hurdle Hops (Sand Pit)
Med Ball Circuit" Little Dude"
Cool Down

Thursday
Jog 800 to 1,200 Meters
Static Stretch/Dynamic Flex/Hurdle Drills/Sprint Drills/5 x 70 m
6 x Resistance Towing
Sprinters & Hurdlers: 7 x 200 Meters (80%) 3mR   "GRASS"
400 Meters: 10 x 200 Meters (80%) 3mR   "GRASS"
Cool Down
Weight Room

Friday
Jog 800 to 1,200 Meters
Static Stretch/Dynamic Flex/Hurdle Drills/Sprint Drills/5 x 70m
Sprinters & Hurdlers: 3 x 350 Meters (80%)   3mR "GRASS"
400 Meters 4 x 350 Meters (80%)   3mR "GRASS"
4 x Body Weight Circuit
Cool Down

Saturday
Rest or Jog 10 minutes and 5 x 100's Grass

Sunday
Jog 15-25 minutes on GRASS

Everyone-Do 2-3 morning runs of 15-20 minutes-EASY*

General Conditioning Training-Week#4
Sprints/Hurdles/Relays

Monday
Jog 800 to 1,200 Meters
Static Stretch/Dynamic Flex/Hurdle Drills/Sprint Drills/5 x 70
SPRINTS: 6 x 300 meters (80%)   3mR "Grass"
HURDLES: 7 x 300 meters (80%)   3mR "Grass"
400 METERS: 8 x 300 meters (80% 3mR   "Grass"
Shot Throws "Gun"

Tuesday
Jog 800 to 1,200 Meters
Static Stretch/Dynamic Flex/Hurdle Drills/Sprint Drills/5 x 70
SPRINTS: 12 x 100's "Grass"
HURDLES: 12 x 100's "Grass"
400 METERS 20 minute Run   6 x 100's "Grass"
Plyometrics: 6 x 5 Double Leg Hurdle Hops (Sand Pit)
Cool Down   Weight Room

Wednesday Jog 800 to 1,200 Meters
Static Stretch/Dynamic Flex/Hurdle Drills/Sprint Drills/5 x 70
Continuous Relay Day   (Do on Track)
(2 Teams) Each Runner on each team runs 5 x 200 meter-relay
 sticks (Timed)

Thursday
Jog 800 to 1,200 Meters
Static Stretch/Dynamic Flex/Hurdle Drills/Sprint Drills/5 x 70 m
SPRINTS: 10 x 100's (75%) "GRASS"
HURDLES: 10 x 100's (75%) "GRASS"
400 METERS 12 x 100 meters (75%) "GRASS"
Cool Down   Weight Room

Friday
Jog 800 to 1,200 Meters
Static Stretch/Dynamic Flex/Hurdle Drills/Sprint Drills/5 x 70 m
SPRINTS: 6 x 150 meters (85%) 3mR "GRASS"
HURDLES: 6 x 150 meters (85%) 3mR "GRASS"
400 METERS: 8 x 150 meters (85%) 3mR "GRASS"
Med Ball "little Dude"
4 x Body weight circuit"

Saturday
Rest or 1 mile and 8 x 100's Grass

Sunday
2 x 3 miles Cross Country   8 x 100's

Everyone-Do 2-3 morning runs of 15-20 minutes-EASY*

EVENT SPECIFIC TRAINING

Event Specific Training
(Sprints/Hurdles/Relays)- Week#1

Monday: Jog 1200 Meters
            Dynamic Flex Drills/Hurdle Drills/Sprint Drills/5 x 70 meters
            SPRINTERS: 350 Meters (85%) 10mR   2 x (50, 50, 50)
            90-95% 3mR 10mR-se
            100 HURDLES: 350 Meters (85%) 10mR 2 x3 Lead/Trail
            5 x5 hurdlers (8.0 m) Apart 3mR- 90%
            HURDLERS: 350 Meters(85%)10mR (10 x 8 High Hurdles) "39"
            80-85%
            WEIGHT ROOM***

Tuesday: Jog 1200 Meters
            Dynamic Flex Drills/Hurdle Drills/Sprint Drills/5 x 70 Meters
            SPRINTERS: 250 Meters (85%)   4 x 150 meters (80%)
                             OR 400 METER RELAY HAND-OFFS
            HURDLERS: 250 Meters (85%) 300 Meter Hurdle Workout
            1 x 5 Hurdles, 1 x 8 hurdles, 3 x 5 Hurdles (All at 80%)

WEDNES: Jog 1200 Meters
            Dynamic Flex Drills/Hurdle Drills/Sprint Drills/5 x 70 meters
            SPRINTERS: 300 Meters (80%)   10mR 4 x 100 Fly's (90-95%)
            100 HURDLERS: 300 Meters (80%) 10mR 10 x 8 Hurdlers (8.0
            meters apart) 3mR 80-85%
            HURDLERS: 300 Meters(85%)10mR 5 X 5 Lead/Trail &10 x 8
            High Hurdles (90%)
            WEIGHT ROOM***

Thursday: Jog 1200 Meters
            Dynamic Flex Drills/Hurdle Drills/Sprint Drills/5 x 70 meters
            SPRINTER: 10 x 100's (75%) GRASS   "Technique"
            HURDLERS: 200 (70%) 300 Hurdle Workout:
            5 x 5 400 Hurdles (80-85%)

Friday: Jog 1200 Meters
            Dynamic Flex/Hurdle Drills/Sprint Drills/5 x 70 meters
            SPRINTERS: 5 x 150 Meters (85%) 4 x 20 meter block Starts
            HURDLERS: 5 x 150 Meters (85%)4 x 1 Hurdles from Blocks

Saturday: 20-30 Minute Run Grass or Trails   or REST

Sunday   15-20 Minute Grass Run Easy 5 x 100's   Flex Drills

Everyone-Do 2-3 morning runs of 15-20 minutes-EASY*

Event Specific Training
(400 Meters/400 Hurdles/800 Meters) Week #1

Monday: Jog 1600-2000 Meters
               Dynamic Flex/Hurdle Drills Sprint Drills/5 x 70 meters
               400 METERS: 500 M. (85%), 300 M. (85%) 250 M(80%)
                        200-(75%)
               400 HURDLERS: 500M (85%),300M (85%), 250M (80%),
                        200-(75%)
               800 METERS:1200 Meters (90%) 6mR, 800(85%)3mR,
               400 (80%) 200 (80%)
               Weight Room-Testing

Tuesday: Jog 1600-2000 Meters
               Dynamic Flex Drills/Hurdle Drills/Sprint Drills/5 x 70 meters
               400 METERS: 3 x 300 Meters "Event Runs"
                        "Sprint-Float-Accelerate" (80-85%)
               400 HURDLERS: 200 (75%) 1 x 5H (85%), 1 x 8 hurdles (85%),
                        3 x 5 (80%)
               800 METERS: 30-40 minute Run 8 x 100's Grass

Wednesday Jog 1600-2000 Meters
               Dynamic Flex/Hurdle Drills/Sprint Drills/ 5 x 70 meters
               400 Meters: 25 Minute Run 10 x 100's Grass "Easy" (70%)
               400 Hurdles: 25 Minute Run 10 x 8 Hurdles (R-L) "4 Step Drill"
               800 Meters: 5 x 250's (80%)   3-4mR
                        Weight Room

Thursday: Jog 1600-2000 Meters
               Dynamic Flex/Hurdle Drills/Sprint Drills/5 x 70 meters
               400 METERS:25-35 Minute Run 10 x 100's (75%) "Grass"
               400 HURDLES: 200 (70%)   5 x 5 Hurdles (80%)
               800 METERS: 30-40 Minute Run   10 x 100's Grass

Friday: Jog 1600-2000 Meters
               Dynamic Flex Drills/Hurdle Drills/Sprint Drills/5 x 70 meters
               400 METERS: 5 x 150's (85%) 4mR
               400 HURDLES: 5 x 150's (85%) 4mR
               800 METERS: 5 x 150's (85%) 4mR

Saturday   Rest or 25-35 minute Run

Sunday   400 Meters & 400 Hurdles 20-25 minute Run   5 x 100's
               800 Meters   40-50 minute Run   5 x 100's

Everyone-Do 1-2 morning runs of 15-20 minutes-EASY***

EVENT SPECIFIC TRAINING
(Sprints/Hurdles/Dual Hurdlers)-Week #2

Monday:
800-1200 Meters Warm-up
Dynamic Flex/Hurdle Drills/Sprint Drills/5 x 70 meters
HURDLERS: 5 x 5 Lead Leg, 5 x 5 Trail Leg
300 Meters 85%, (10-15mR) 10 x 5 hurdles (8.5m) 85-90%
100 HURDLERS: 300 Meters 85%, 2 x 3 hurdles Lead/Trail Leg
4 x 10 hurdles (8.0 meters apart) 3mR 85-90%
SPRINTERS: (300 Meters 85%) 10-15mR 2 x 60m,70m,80m
"Speed I" at 95%   3mR 8-10M Sets

Tuesday
800-1200 Warm-up Jog
Dynamic Flex/Hurdle Drills/Sprint Drills/5 x 70 meters
12 x 100 Meters 75% "GRASS"   Technique
Plyometrics: "Plyo Jam"
WEIGHT ROOM

Wednesday 800-1200 Meter Warm-up
Dynamic Flex/Hurdle Drills/Sprint Drills/5 x 70 meters
HURDLERS: 200 (75%)   6 x 5 IH Hurdles (85%)   200 (75%)
SPRINTERS: 300 (80%)250(80) 200 (80) 200(75%) 100(70%)

Thursday
800-1200 Warm-up Jog
Dynamic Flex Drills/Hurdle Drills/Sprint Drills/5 x 70 meters
10 x 100 Strides (70-75%) "GRASS"
Plyometrics: 5 x 5 Double Leg Hurdle Hops (Sand)
Weight Room

Friday
800-1200 Warm-up Jog
Dynamic Flex/Hurdle Drills/Sprint Drills/ 5 x 70 meters
HURDLERS: 100 meters (75%)5 x 5 hurdles (Lead/Trail Leg)
12 x 5 hurdles (8.5 meters apart)85%
100 HURDLES:100 (75%) 5 x 5 Lead/Trail leg)10 x 6 hurdles
(8 meters apart) 85%
SPRINTERS:2 x 150,150,150(85%)3mR & 8-10 M rest @sets

Saturday
Sprinters & Hurdlers: 20-30 minute Run-Easy 5 x 100 strides

Sunday
Sprinters & Hurdlers: 18-25 minute Run Easy 6 x 100
WEIGHT ROOM

1-2 morning runs of 15-20 minutes-EASY***

Event Specific Training
(400, 300 Hurdles & 800 Meters)-Week #2

Monday   1600-2000 Warm-up
            Dynamic Flex Drills, Hurdle Drills, Sprint Drills.5 x 70 meters
            800 METERS: 1200Meters (90%)4mR 600(85%)3mR 500 (85%) 3mR
                    400(85%)
            400 M/ 300 HURDLERS: 500 (90%) 400 (85%)300 (80%) 2 x 200(75%)
            Cool Down

Tuesday   800 METERS: 25-30 Minute Run   10 x 100's grass
            400 METERS & 300 HURDLERS: 25 Minute Run   10 x 100's Grass
            Plyometrics: Big Sandy Circuit
            WEIGHT ROOM

Wednesday   1200 meters-1600 meters Warm-up
            Dynamic Flex, Hurdle Drills, Sprint Drills, 5 x 70 meters
            800 METERS: 600 Meters (85%) 4mR 5 x 200 (75%) 2mR@
            300 HURDLERS: 200(75%) 6 x 5 IH hurdles(85%) 200 (75%)
            400 METERS: 600(90%) 4mR,   5 x 200 Meters (75%) 100walk
            800 Meter Cool-down

Thursday   800 METERS: 25-30 minutes Run   5 x 100's "Grass"
            400 METERS/400 IH   20-30 Minute Run 5 x 100's "Grass"
            WORKOUT   10 x 100's Grass Strides build-ups
            Plyometrics: 6 x 5 Double Leg Hurdle Hops (Sand)
            Weight Room

Friday   1200-1600 Warm-up
            800 METERS: 6 x 300 Meters (80%) 100 Meter Jog@ own
            400 METERS/300 IH   8 x 200 meters (80%) 3-4 mR@
            800 Meter Cool Down

Saturday   800 METERS: 30-40 Minute long run-EASY 5 x 100's Grass
            400 METERS & -300 HURDLERS: 20-25 Minute Run   5 x 100's Grass

Sunday   800 Meters 20-25 Minute Run
            400 & 300 IH   20-25 Minute Run

Do Morning runs 15-25 minutes-EASY (3-Days a week)

Event Specific Training
Sprints, Hurdles & Relays-Week #3

Monday: 800-1200 Meter Jog
               Dynamic Stretch/Hurdle Drills/Sprint Drills/5 x 70 meters
               (Everyone) 300 Meters (90%)   10 min Recovery
               Sprinters: 300 (90%) 2(90m, 100m, 110m) at (90-95%)3 min rest 8m sets
               Hurdlers: 300 (90%) 5 x 5 hurdles (Lead/Trail) 6 x 60 over Hurdles 90-95%
               (36 inches) 3 min Rest @ 8-10 minutes Sets
               100 HURDLERS: 300(85%) 5 x 5 lead/Trail leg 6 x 5 hurdles(8.5M) 90-95%
               3 minute Rest@ 8-10 minute rest for sets

Tuesday: 800-1200 Meter Warm-up
               Dynamic Flex Drills/Hurdle Drills/Sprint Drills/5 x 70 meters
               2 x 100 meter Strides (70-75%) GRASS "Technique"
               Weight Room

Wednesday   800-1200 meter Jog
               Dynamic Flex/Hurdle Drills/Sprint Drills/5 x 70 meters
               SPRINTERS: 300 (85%) 250 Meters (80%) 200 Meters(75%)
               200 meters (75%) 150 Meters (75%)
               HURDLERS: 250 meters (75%) 6 x 5 300 M. Hurdles (85%)
               Overhead Shot Throws x 4

Thursday: 800-1200 Meter Jog
               Dynamic Flex Drills/Hurdle Drills/Sprint Drills/5 x 70 meters
               Everyone: 10 x 100 Meter Stride Build-ups   (75%) "GRASS"
               Weight Room

Friday: 800-1200 Meter Jog
               Dynamic Flex Drills/Hurdle Drills/Sprint Drills/5 x 70 meters
               Sprinters: 250 (85%) 250 (85%) 3 x 200 meters (75%)
               Hurdlers: 250 (75%) 5 x 5 Hurdles (Lead/Trail Leg)
                            2 x (6 x 6 Hurdles) (8.5 meters apart)   80%
               100 HURDLERS: 5 x 5 Lead/Trail Leg 2 x 5 x 5 hurdles (8.0m apart) 80%

Saturday   20-30 minute Run-Easy

Sunday   15-20 Minute Run EASY (8 x 100 strides)
                            WEIGHT ROOM

2-3 days a week do a 15-20 minute run in morning

EVENT SPECIFIC TRAINING
(400 Meters, 300 Hurdles & 800 Meters)-Week #3

Monday:
800-1200 Meter Warm-up
Dynamic Flex Drills/Hurdle Drills/Sprint Drills/5 x70 meters
400 METERS: 450 Meters (90%), 300 meters (85%), 250 meters (85%),
200 Meters (75%), 150 Meters (75%)
800 METERS: 1,200 meters (90%), 5mR 600 meters (85%), 4mR
300 (80%), (2mR) 200 (75%)

Tuesday
800-1200 Meter jog
Dynamic Flex Drills/Hurdle Drills/Sprints Drills/5 x 70 meters
400 METERS & 300 HURDLERS: *20-30 minute run 8 x 100 strides*
800 METERS: *40-45 Minute Run   8 x 100's GRASS*
** WEIGHT ROOM:

Wednesday
800-1200 Meter Jog
Dynamic Flex Drills/Hurdle Drills/Sprints Drills/5 x 70 meters
400 METERS: 500 Meters (90%), 400 Meters(85%), 300 meters (80%)
          1 x 150 meters (75%)
300 HURDLES: 250 Meters (70%)   6 x 5 300 Hurdles (80-85%)
800 METERS: 3 x 400 Meters (80-85%) 4 M Rest "RACE PACE"

Thursday
800-1200 Meter Jog
Dynamic Flex Drills/Hurdle Drills/Sprints Drills/5 x 70 meters
400 METERS: 300 Hurdles-25-30 minute Run 8 x 100's
800 METERS: 25-30 minute Run   6 x 100 Strides   GRASS
**WEIGHT ROOM

Friday
800-1200 meter warm-up
Dynamic Flex Drills/Hurdle Drills/Sprints Drills/5 x 70 meters
400 METERS/300 Hurdles: 2x(150,150,150,150)85% 3 min @8 mR sets
800 METERS: 1000 meters (90%) 4mR
8 x 200 meters (70-75%) 90 second Recovery

Saturday
400 & 300 HURDLERS: 35-40 minute run-Easy
800 METERS: 20-30 Minute Run-EASY

Sunday
400 METERS & 300 HURDLES: 20-30 minute run   5 x 100's
800 meter Runners: 20-30 minute run Easy   5 x 100's!

Everyone-Do 3-4 morning runs of 15-20 minutes-EASY*

EVENT SPECIFIC TRAINING
(Sprints, Hurdles & Relays)-Week #4

Monday: 800-1200 Meter Jog
Dynamic Flex Drills/Hurdle Drills/Sprint Drills/5 x 70 meters
Sprinters: 300 meters (85-90%) 2 (50,50 50 Meters) 90-95% 3mR 8-10MrS
Hurdlers: 300 Meters (85-90%) 2 x 10 Kick-Catch Drill, 5 x 5 Lead/Trail Drill
10 x 5 hurdles (80-85%) 3min Rest   (39 inches)
100 HURDLERS: 300 (85%-90%) 2 x 10 Kick-Catch Drill 5 x 5 Lead/Trail
Leg 10 x 5 Hurdles (Normal distance) 80-85% 3mR@

Tuesday   800-1200 Meter Jog
Dynamic Flex Drills/Hurdle Drills/Sprint Drills/ 5 x70 meters
SPRINTERS: 5 x 200 meters (80%) seconds   3mR
300 HURLERS   200 (70%)   5 x 5 IH Hurdles (80-85%) 3mR
** WEIGHT ROOM

Wednesday 800-1200 Meters Jog
Dynamic Flex Drills/Hurdle Drills/Sprint Drills/5 x 70 meters
15 minute Run
12 x 100 Stride Build-ups (80%) " Technique"

Thursday 800-1200 Meters
Dynamic Flex Drills/Hurdle Drills/Sprint Drills/5 x 70 meters
Sprinters: 5 x 150 meters (85%)
Hurdlers: 5 x 5 Lead/Trail Leg 200 (70%) 10 x 5 Hurdles (80-85%)
100 HURDLERS: 5 x 5 Lead/Trail leg, 200(70%) 10 x 5hurdles 8.0m's (90%)
       ** WEIGHT ROOM

Friday   800-1200 Meters
Dynamic Flex Drills/Hurdle Drills/Sprint Drills/5 x 70 meters
Sprinters: 300 (80%) 4 x 100 "Flys" (90-95%)
Hurdlers: 300 (80%) 4 x 100 "Flys" (90-95%)

Saturday 15-20 minute Run-Flexibility

Sunday   Rest or 15-20 minute Run-Easy

Do 2-3 morning runs of 15-20 minutes each day

EVENT SPECIFIC TRAINING
(400 Meters, 300 hurdles & 800 meters)-Week #4

Monday: 1600-2000 Meter Jog
               Dynamic Flex /Hurdle Drills/Sprint Drills/5 x 70 meters
               800 METERS: 1000 Meters (90%)   4 x 200 (85%) 2mR
               400 METERS/400 Hurdlers: 500 meters (90%) 6mR, 300 Meters (85%)
               4mR, 250 meters (85%) 3mR 200 Meters (80%)

Tuesday   1600-2000 Meter Jog
               Dynamic Flex Drills/Hurdle Drills/Sprint Drills/5 x 70 meters
               400 Meters: 20-25 Minute run   10 x 100 strides "GRASS"
               800 Meters: 25-30 Minute run   10 x 100 strides "GRASS"
                     ** WEIGHT ROOM

Wednesday 1600-2000 Meter Jog
               Dynamic Flex Drills/Hurdle Drills/Sprint Drills/5 x 70 meters
               800 METERS: 3 x 600M (85%) 4m.Rest @ 8-10mR then 3x 200 (75%)
               300 Meter Hurdles: 200 Meters (70%) 5 x 5 hurdles (85%) 3mR
                400 Meters   5 x 300 meters (85%) 4min Rest Each

Thursday   1600-2000 Meter Jog
               Dynamic Flex Drills/Hurdle Drills/Sprint Drills/5 x 70 meters
               400 Meters   20-25 minute run   8 x 100 Strides "GRASS"
               800 Meters   30-35 minute run   8 x 100 Strides "GRASS"
               ** WEIGHT ROOM

Friday   1600-2000 Meter Jog
               Dynamic Flex/Hurdle Drills/Sprint Drills/5 x 70 meters
               800 METERS: 6 x 150 Meters (85%) 3 min Rest
               400 METERS & 300 IH   6 x 150 Meters (85%) 3 min Rest

Saturday   400 Meters: 20-25 minute Run   5 x 100 strides "GRASS"
               800 METERS: 25-35 minute Run 5 x 100 strides "GRASS"

Sunday   400 METERS: 20-25 minute run   6 x 100's
               800 METERS: 25-35 minute run   6 x 100's

Everyone: Do-Easy Morning Runs of 20-25 minutes 3-4 mornings**

EVENT SPECIFIC TRAINING
(Sprints, Hurdles & Relays)-Week #5

Monday   Jog 1200-1600 Meters
            Dynamic Flex/Hurdle Drills/Sprint Drills/5 x 70 meters
            SPRINTERS: 300 meters (85%) 10mR 2 x 60,70,80 meters (90-95%) 3mR
            HURDLERS: 300 meters (85%) 10mR 2 x 60,70,80 meters (90-95%) 3mR

Tuesday   Jog 1200-1600 meters
            Dynamic Flex Drills/Hurdle Drills/Sprint Drills/5 x 70 meters
            SPRINTERS: 6 x 200 meters (70%) 200 meter walk
            HURDLERS: 3 x 10 Kick Catch Drill 5 x 5 Lead/trail legs
            200 meters (70%) 12 x 5 hurdles (39inches) 80-85%
            100 HURDLERS: 200(70%) 10 x 5 hurdles (8.0 meters apart) 80-85%
                        *** WEIGHT ROOM

Wednesday   Jog 1200-1600 Meter Jog
            Dynamic Flex Drills/Hurdle Drills/Sprint Drills/5 x 70 meters
            12 x 100 strides (70%) GRASS
            Plyometrics: 6 x 5 Double Leg Hurdle Hops

Thursday   Jog 1200-1600 Meters
            Dynamic Flex Drills/Hurdle Drills/Sprint Drills/5 x 70 meters
            SPRINTERS: 300 Meters (85%)   4 x 150 meters (80%)
            HURDLERS: 300 Meters (85%)   5 x 5 Lead/Trail Leg
            300 Hurdle Workout- 2 x 8 hurdles, 2 x 6 hurdles, 3 x 3 hurdles (80-85%)
                        ***WEIGHT ROOM

Friday   Jog 1200-1600 Meters
            Dynamic Flex Drills/Hurdle Drills/Sprint Drills/5 x 70 meters
            SPRINTERS: 3 x 100 Curves 5 x 20 meter-Blocks 90-95%
            HURDLERS: 2 x 100 Curves 4 x 1H, 3x 2H, 1x 3H   90-95%
            100 HURDLERS: 2 x 100 Curves 4 x 1H, 2 x2H, 3 x1H 90-95%
                        # 1,600 Relay Hand-off's & 5

Saturday   **TRACK MEET**

Sunday   Jog 20-25 Minutes
            Flexibility Drills   8 x 100's Strides

*** EVERYONE: Do 2-3 Morning Runs of 15-20 minutes ****

EVENT SPECIFIC TRAINING
400 Meters, 300 Hurdles & 800 Meters-Week #5

Monday   Jog 1600-2000 Meters
            Dynamic flex Drills/Hurdle Drills/Sprint Drills/ 5 x 70 meters
            800 METERS: 1200 Meters (85%) 4mR, 800 Meters:(85%) 4mR,
                        400 Meters (80%) 3mR 200 (75%)
            400 METERS/300 Hurdles: 450 Meters (85%) 300 Meters (85%)
                        250 Meters (80%) 2 X 200 Meters (75%)

Tuesday   Jog 1600-2000 meters
            Dynamic Flex Drills/Hurdle Drills/Sprint Drills/5 x 70 meters
            800 METERS: 12 x 200 Meters (75%) with 100 meter jog
            400 METERS: 8 x 200 Meters (75%) with 200 meter walk
            300 HURDLES: 200 (70%) 8 x 5 Hurdles (75%) with 200 walk
            ***Weights

Wednesday   400/300 Hurdlers: 20-25 minutes   10 x 100's
            800 Meters: 20-30 minutes   10 x 100's

Thursday   Jog 1600-2000 Meters
            Dynamic Flex Drills/Hurdle Drills/Sprint Drills/5 x 70 meters
            800 METERS: 4 x 400 Meters 85% (Race Pace)   5mR
            400 METERS: 500 meters (85%) 5mR 4 x 200 meters(75%)
            ***Weights

Friday   Jog 1600-2000 Meters
            "PRE-MEET WARM-UP"
            Dynamic Flex Drills/Hurdle Drills/Sprint Drills/5 x 70 meters
            400 Meters   3 x 100   "CURVES FROM BLOCKS HARD-Break Point"
            300 Hurdlers: 3 x 1 Hurdle, 2 x 2 hurdles "Race effort"
            800 Meters: 5 x 100's "CURVES"& Break Point
            ###1,600 Relay Hand-Off's X 5

Saturday   **TRACK MEET**

Sunday   800 Meters: 25-35 Minute Run
            400 Meters: 20-30 minutes run

Everyone: Do 2-3 Morning Runs of 20-30 minutes-EASY

EVENT SPECIFIC TRAINING
(Sprint, Hurdles & Relays)-Week #6

Monday
Jog 800-1200 meters
Dynamic Flex Drills/Hurdle Drills/Sprint Drills 5 x 70 meters
SPRINTERS & HURDLERS: 300 meters (85%)   10min Rest
2 x (100,110,120) 90-95%   3mR   8 Min Rest between sets
**** Weight Room

Tuesday
Jog 800-1200 meters
Dynamic Flex Drills/Hurdles Drills/Sprint Drills/5 x 70 meters
SPRINTERS: 400(85%) 300(85%) 250(80%) 200(75%) 150 (75%)
HURDLERS: 200 meters (75%) 3 x 10 Kick-Catch Drill, 5 x 5 lead/Trail
2 (5 x 5 Hurdles) 39 inches (80-85%) 3 min rest@ 8-10m. sets
100 HURDLERS:2(5 x 5 Hurdles) 7.5 meters apart   3mR@8-10mR sets

Wednesday
Jog 800-1600 meters
Dynamic Flex Drills/Hurdle Drills/Sprint Drills/5 x 70 meters
SPRINTERS: 12 x 100 Strides (Grass)
HURDLERS: 200 (70%)   300 Meter Hurdles: 5 x 5H (Race Effort))
***WEIGHT ROOM

Thursday
Jog 1200-1600 meters
Dynamic Flex Drills/Hurdle Drills/Sprint Drills/5 x 70 meters
HURDLERS: 3 x 10 Kick-Catch Drill, 5 x 5 Lead/Trail Leg 150 meters (80%)
2 x (5H, 5H,5H,5H) (85%) 3 m. rest@ 8-10 m. Sets
SPRINTERS: 300 meters (85%)   4 x 200 meters (75%)

Friday
Jog 1200-1600 meters
Dynamic Flex Drills/Hurdle Drills/Sprint Drills/5 x 70 meters
SPRINTERS: 2 x 150 meters (75%)3mR   4 x 20 meter Block Starts
HURDLERS: 2 x 150 meters (75%) 3mR   3 x 1 Hurdles, 2 x 2 hurdles
100 HURDLERS: 2 x 150 meters (75%) 3mR   3 x 1 hurdles, 2 x 2 hurdles

Saturday
TRACK MEET

Sunday:
Distance Run 15-20 minutes, Flexibility Drills
          5 x 100 strides

Do Morning Runs of 15-20 minutes 2-3 days a week!

EVENT SPECIFIC TRAINING
(400, 300 Hurdles, 800 meters) -Week #6

Monday
Jog 1600-2000 meters
Dynamic Flex/ Hurdle Drills/Sprint Drills/5 x 70 meters
800 METERS: 1000 Meters(85%) 6mR 600 Meters (85%) 5mR,
4 x 200's (75%) 2mR
400 METERS: 500 Meters (85%), 300 Meters (85%)
250 Meters (75%), 200 Meters (70%)

Tuesday
Jog 1600-2000 meters
Dynamic Flex/ Hurdle Drills/Sprint Drills/5 x 70 m
800 METERS: 30-35 minute run 5 x 100's "Grass"
400 METERS: 20-30 minute run 5 x 100s' "Grass"
#1,600 Meter Relay Sticks
WEIGHT ROOM

Wednesday
Jog 1600-2000 meters
Dynamic Flex Drills/hurdler Drills/Sprint Drills/5 x 70 meters
800 METERS: 5 x 300 Meters (80-85%)3mR
400 METERS: 5 x 300 meters (80-85%)3mR
400 HURDLES 200(70%) 6 x 5 hurdles (80-85%) 1 x 300 (75%)

Thursday
Jog 1600-2000 meters
Dynamic Flex/ Hurdle Drills/Sprint Drills/5 x 70 meters
800 METERS: 30-35 minute run 6 x 100's
400 METERS: 20-25 minute run 6 x 100's
WEIGHT ROOM

Friday
Jog 1600-2000 meters
Dynamic Flex /Hurdle Drills/Sprint Drills/5 x 70 meters
800 METERS: 4 x 200 meters (Race Pace)
400 METERS: 2 x (150)3mR (85%) 4 x 20 meter Block Starts
300 HURDLERS: 150(80%) 4 x 1 hurdles, 2 x 2 hurdles from Blocks

Saturday
TRACK MEET

Sunday
800 METERS 30-35 minute Run   5 x 100's
400 METERS: 20-25 minute run   5 x 100's

EVERYONE: Do Morning Runs of 15-25 minutes 3 days a week****

EVENT SPECIFIC TRAINING
(Sprints, Hurdles & Relays)-Week #7

Monday
Jog 1200-1600 meters
Dynamic Flex/Hurdle Drills/Sprint Drills/5 x 70 meters
SPRINTERS: 300 Meters (85%) 2 (50,50,50,50) 90-95% 3mR   10mR sets
HURDLERS: 300 Meters (85%) 2 (5H,5H,5H) 90-95% 3mR   10mR-Sets
100 HURDLERS 300 Meters (85%) 5 x 5 lead/Trail Leg
                        2 (5H,5H,5H) 7.5 meters apart 3mR 10mR sets
***WEIGHT ROOM

Tuesday
Jog 1200-1600 Meters
Dynamic Flex Drills/Hurdle Drills/Sprint Drills/5 x 70 meters
SPRINTERS: 4 x 250 Meters 80-85% 4mR
HURDLERS: 4 x 250 Meters 80-85% 4mR
#1,600 Relay Hand-off's X 5

Wednesday
Jog 1200-1600 Meters
Dynamic Flex Drills/Hurdle Drills/Sprint Drills/5 x 70 meters
SPRINTERS: 5 x 60 Meter "Flys" (90-95%)
HURDLERS: 1 x 60 Meter "Fly" (90-95%) 5 x 5 Lead Trail/Leg
1 (5H,5H,5H) (8.5 meters apart) 36 inches 1 x 60 Meter "Fly"(90%)
100 HURDLERS 1 x 60M Fly (90-95%)   5 x 5 Lead/Trail Leg
1 x (5H, 5H,5H) 7.5 meters apart (85-90%) 3mR@ 10mR-sets
                        WEIGHT ROOM

Thursday
JOG 1200-1600 Meters
Dynamic Flex Drills/Hurdle Drills/Sprint Drills/5 x 70 meters
SPRINTERS: 12 x 100 Meters "Grass" (70-75%)
HURDLERS: 12 x 100 Meters "Grass" (70-75%)
#1,600 Meter Relay Han-off's x 5

Friday
Pre Meet Warm-up
Jog 800-1200 Meters
Dynamic Flex Drills/Hurdle Drills/Sprint Drills/5 x 70 meters
SPRINTERS: 3 x 100 Curves, 5 x 20 meter-Blocks 95%
HURDLERS: 2 x 100 Curves, 4 x 1H, 3x 2H, 1x 3H 95%
100 HURDLERS: 2 x 100 Curves, 4 x 1H, 2 x2H, 3 x1H 95%
 # 1,600 Relay Hand-off's & 5

Saturday   **TRACK MEET**

Sunday   Rest or 20-25 Minute Jog 5 x 100's Grass

** Do 2 morning distance runs of 12-15 minutes followed by stretching**

EVENT SPECIFIC TRAINING
(400, 300 Hurdles & 800 Meters)-Week #7

Monday
Jog 1600-2000 Meters
Dynamic Flex/Hurdle Drills/Sprint Drills/5 x 70 meters
800 METERS: 1000 meters(90%) 8mR, 600 Meters (85%)5mR
400 meters (80%) 4mR, 200 Meters (75%)
400 METERS: 600 Meters (90%) 300 Meters (85%)
2 x 200 Meters (80%)
****Weight Room

Tuesday
Jog 1600-2000 Meters
Dynamic Flex/Hurdle Drills/Sprint Drills/5 x 70 meters
800 METERS: 5 x 250   Meters (85%) 3mR@
400 METERS: 4 x 250   Meters (85%) 3mR@
300 HURDLES: 1 x 8 Hurdles (90%), 3 x 5 Hurdles (90%)
#1,600 Meter Relay Hand-Off's x 5

Wednesday
Jog 1600-2000 Meters
Dynamic Flex Drills/Hurdle Drills/Sprint Drills/5 x 70 meters
800 METERS: 3 x 400 Meters (85%)   4 Min Rest   "Race pace"
400 METERS: 300 Meters (85%) 8mR 3 x 150's (80%)   4mR
300 HURDLERS: Same as 400 meters
Weight Room*

Thursday
800 METERS   30-40 minute Run   6 x 100's Strides
400 METERS: 20-30 minute Run   6 x 100's strides
#1,600 Meter Relay Hand-offs   X 5

Friday
Jog 1600-2000 Meters
"PRE-MEET WARM-UP"
Dynamic Flex Drills/Hurdle Drills/Sprint Drills/5 x 70 meters
400 Meters   3 x 100   "CURVES FROM BLOCKS HARD-Break Point"
300 Hurdlers: 3 x 1 Hurdle, 2 x 2 hurdles
800 Meters: 5 x 100's "CURVES"& Break Point
###1,600 Relay Hand-Off's X 5

Saturday
TRACK MEET

Sunday
15-25 minute distance Run 5 x 100's GRASS

EVERYONE ** Do 2-3 Morning runs of 15-25 minutes this week*

EVENT SPECIFIC TRAINING
(Sprints, Hurdles & Relays)-Week #8

Monday   Jog 800-1200 Meters
            Dynamic Flex/Hurdle Drills/Sprint Drills 5 x 70 meters
            SPRINTERS: 300 Meters (85%)10mR, 2x (60,70,80) 90-95% 3mR, 10mR
                       sets
            HURDLERS: 300 Meters (85%)10mR, 2 x (60,70,80) 90-95%3mR, 10mR
            WEIGHT ROOM

Tuesday   Jog 800-1200 Meters
            Dynamic Flex/Hurdle Drills/Sprint Drills/5 x 70 meters
            SPRINTERS: 4 x 250 Meters (85%) 4mR
            HURDLERS: 2 x 10 Kick-Catch, 5 x 5 Lead/Trail leg 250 METERS (75%)
                      2 x (8H, 8H, 8H) 39inches 90-95% 3Mr @ 8-10 Min Rest sets
            100 HURDLERS: 250 (75%) 4 x 5 lead/Trail Leg   2 x 8H (8.0 meters apart)
                          90-95% 3mR

Wednesday   Jog 800-1200 Meters
            Dynamic Flex Drills/Hurdle Drills/Sprint Drills/5 x 70 meters
            SPRINTERS: 12 x 100's Strides (70%) EASY   GRASS
            HURDLERS: 12 x 100's Strides (70%) EASY   GRASS
            #1,600 Relay Hand-Offs x 5
            *** WEIGHT ROOM****

Thursday   Jog 800-1200 Meters
            Dynamic Flex Drills/Hurdle Drills/Sprint Drills/5 x 70 meters
            SPRINTERS: 250 (70%) 5 x 20 meter block starts
            HURDLERS: 2 x 10 Kick-Catch, 5 x 5 Lead/Trail   250 (70%)
            4 x 1 Hurdle, 3 x 2 hurdles, 3 x 3 hurdles (90-95%) From Blocks
            100 HURLERS: Same as Above

Friday   Pre Meet Warm-up
            Jog 800-1200 Meters
            Dynamic Flex Drills/Hurdle Drills/Sprint Drills/5 x 70 meters
            SPRINTERS: 3 x 100's   5 x 20 meter-Blocks 90-95%
            HURDLERS: 2 x 100 's   4 x 1H, 3x 2H, 1x 3H 90-95%
            100 HURDLERS: 2 x 100's 4 x 1H, 3 x 2H, 1 x 3H 90-95%
            # 1,600 Relay Hand-off's & 5

Saturday   **TRACK MEET**

Sunday   Distance Run of 20-25 minutes

      ** Do 2 morning runs of 15-20 minutes with stretching**

EVENT SPECIFIC TRAINING
(400 Meters, 300 Hurdles & 800 Meters)-Week #8

Monday
1600-2000 Meters
Dynamic Flex/Hurdle Drills/Sprint Drills/5 x 70 meters
800 METERS: 600 Meters (90%) 5mR   4 x 200 M (75%) 60sec R
300 HURDLERS/400 METERS: 450 Meters (90%), 8mR
                                         300M (85%) 6mR, 200 (85%)
WEIGHT ROOM

Tuesday
1600-2000 Meters
Dynamic Flex/Hurdle Drills/Sprint Drills/5 x 70 meters
800 METERS: 25-30 Minute Run   6 x 100's   GRASS
300 HURDLERS/ 400 METERS: 18-30 Minutes Run   6 x 100's   GRASS
1,600 Relay Hand-offs X 5

Wednesday
1600-2000 Meters
Dynamic Flex/Hurdle Drills/Sprint Drills/ 5 x 70 meters
800 METERS: 4 x 250 Meters (85%)   3mR   5 x 20M Blocks
400 METERS: 4 x 250 Meters (85%)   3mR   5 x 20M Blocks
300 HURDLERS   150 (75%) 4 x 5 Hurdles (80%) from Blocks

Thursday
800 METERS: 20-30 Minute Run   6 x 100's Grass (75%)
400 METERS: 18-25 Minute Run   6 x 100's Grass (75%)
1,600 Relay Hand-Off's X 5

Friday
"PRE-MEET WARM-UP"
Dynamic Flex Drills/Hurdle Drills/Sprint Drills/5 x 70 meters
400 Meters: 4 x 100 "Break Point"
300 Hurdlers: 3 x 1 Hurdle, 2 x 2 hurdles
800 Meters: 6 x 100's "CURVES"& Break Point
###1,600 Relay Hand-Off's X 5

Saturday
TRACK MEET

Sunday:
800 METERS: 40-50 minute run   6 x 100's
400 METERS: 30-35 minute run   6 x 100's

Do 2-3 Morning Runs this week of 15 to 30 minutes each

Event Specific Training
(Sprints, Hurdles, Relays)-Week #9

Monday Jog 1200 Meters
        Dynamic Flex Drills/Hurdle Drills/Sprint Drills/5 x 70 meters
        SPRINTERS:350 Meters(90%)10mR 1 x 150,150,150meters (90-95%)
        HURDLERS: 350 Meters: (90%)10mR 5 x 5 Lead/Trail Leg
                2 x (10H,10H,10H) (36 inches) (90-95%)
        100 HURDLERS: 350 (90%) 10mR 2 x 10H,10H,10H (8m. apart)
        (90-95%)
        ****400 METER RELAY STICK***
        ****WEIGHT ROOM*****

Tuesday Jog 1200 Meters
        Dynamic Flex Drills/Hurdle Drills/Sprint Drills/5 x 70 Meters
        SPRINTERS: 300(85%) 250 (85%) 150(85%) 100(85%)
        400 Meter Relay Stick
        HURDLERS: 150(75%) 2x8-300Hurdles(85%) 3 x2 hurdles (Race Pace)
        400 METER RELAY STICK**

Wednesday Jog 1200 Meters
        Dynamic Flex Drills/Hurdle Drills/Sprint Drills/5 x 70 meters
        SPRINTERS: 3-4 x 100 Meter "Fly's" (90-95%)400 Meter Relay "Stick"
        HURDLERS: 20 minute Run   8 x 100's "GRASS"   OR
                5 x 5 Lead/Trail Leg-5 x 5 Hurdles (90-95%)
        ****400 METER RELAY WORKOUT***
        ****WEIGHT WORKOUT****

Thursday Jog 1200 Meters
        Dynamic Flex Drills/Hurdles Drills/Sprint Drills/5 x 70 meters
        SPRINTERS: 16 x 100's (GRASS)
        HURDLERS: 100 (70%) 1 x 9 H "300 hurdles" & "Sprint" Home (90%)
                1 x 5H, 3mR,1 x 3 H (Race Pace)

Friday Jog 1200 Meters
        Dynamic Flex Drills/Hurdles Drills/Sprint Drills/5 x 70 meters
        SPRINTERS: 100(80%)   6 x 20 meter Block starts
        HURDLERS: 100(80%)   3 x1H, 2 x2H (Both Hurdles)
        100 HURDLERS: 100(80%) 3 x1H, 2 x 2H (Both Hurdles)

Saturday **TRACK MEET**

Sunday 15-20 Minute Run (6 x 100's)

Do 2-3 morning Runs of 15-20 minutes & Flexibility Drills

Event Specific Training
(400 Meters, 300 Hurdles & 800 Meters)-Week #9

Monday
Jog 1600-2000 Meters
Dynamic Flex Drills/Hurdle Drills/Sprint Drills/5 x 70 meters
400 METERS: 550 Meters (85%) 300 (85%) 2 x 200 (80%)
300 HURDLES: 550 Meters (85%) 300 (85%) 2 x200 (80%)
800 METERS: 1000 Meters: (85%)8mR, 600 Meters(85%) 5MR
 400 Meters(85%)3mR,300 Meters (80%) 3mR, 200 Meters (75%)
****WEIGHTS*****

Tuesday
Jog 1600-2000 Meters
Dynamic Flex/Hurdle Drills/Sprint Drills/5 x 70 meters
400 METERS: 5 x 150's (80-85%)   *** 400 Meter STICK****
300 HURDLES: 150 (70%)2 x 8 Hurdles (85%) 3 x 2H (Race Effort)
800 METERS: 25-35 Minute Run 8 x 100's "Grass or Turf"

Wednesday Jog 1600-2000 Meters
Dynamic Flex/Hurdle Drills/Sprint Drills/5 x 70 meters
400 METERS: 20-30 Minute Run 10 x 100's "Grass or Turf"
300 HURDLES: 20-30 Minute Run 10 x 100's "Grass or Turf"
800 METERS: 600 Meters (95%) 5mR 5 x 200 (75%)
#1,600 Relay Sticks
 ****WEIGHTS****

Thursday
Jog 1200-2000 Meters
Dynamic Flex/Hurdle Drills/Sprint Drills/5 x 70 meters
400 METERS: 4 x 300 Meter "Event" Runs 5mR
 (Sprint 150,Float 50, Sprint 100)
300 HURDLERS: 100 (70%) 1 x 9 hurdles=Sprint Home (10mR)
 1 x 5 hurdles, 2 x 3 hurdles
800 METERS: 35-40 Minute Run, 6 x 100 Strides "GRASS or TURF"

Friday
Jog 1600-200 Meters
Dynamic Flex/Hurdle Drills/Sprint Drills/5 x 70 meters
400 METERS: 2(100,100,100) "FLYS" (90%) 3mR 8-10mR for sets
400 HURDLES:2 (100,100,100) "FLYS" (90%)3mR 8-10mR for sets
800 METERS: 2(100,100,100) "FLYS" (90%)3mR 8-10mR for sets
WEIGHTS*

Saturday
30-50 minute Run Trails (Easy)   Flexibility Drills

Sunday
25-45 minutes Run-Trails (Easy) 4 x 100's

***REAL ATHLETES-Must Do Morning Runs of 18-25 minutes Easy!!!!*

Event Specific Training
(SPRINTS, HURDLES & RELAYS) Week #10

Monday
Jog 1200 Meters
Dynamic Flex/Hurdle Drills/Sprint Drills/5 x 70 meters
SPRINTERS: 300 Meters (85%)1 x (50,50,50,50)90-95% BLOCKS
HURDLERS: 300 Meters (85%) 5 x 5 Lead/Trail Leg
1 x (10H, 10H, 10H) (8.5 Meters) 39 inches 90-95%
100 HURDLERS: 1 x 10H,10H,10H (7.5 Meters apart) 90-95%
##WEIGHTS##

Tuesday
Jog 1200 Meters
Dynamic Flex/Hurdle Drills/Sprint Drills/5 x 70 meters
SPRINTERS: 4 x 250 meters (80%)   3 Min Rest
HURDLERS: 300 Hurdles (100) 75% 1 x 8H, 1 x 5H 2x 3 Hurdles
*** 4 x 100 Meter Relay Hand-off's

Wednesday Jog 1200 Meters
Dynamic Flex/Hurdle Drills/Sprint Drills/5 x 70 meters
SPRINTERS: 2 x 150 meters (85%) 4 x 20 meter block Starts
HURDLERS: 200 (75%)110H's: 3 x 1H, 2 x 2H, 3 x 3H (Race Effort)
100 HURDLERS   Same as above
WEIGHTS***

Thursday
Jog 1200 Meters
Dynamic Flex\Hurdle Drills/Sprint Drills/ 5 x 70 meters
SPRINTERS: 12 x 100's (70%)"GRASS"
HURDLERS: 12 x 100's (70%) GRASS"
 *** 400 METER Relay Hand-off's

Friday
Jog 1200 Meters
Dynamic Flex/Hurdle Drills/Sprint Drills/5 x70 meters
SPRINTERS:2 x 50 meter "Fly's" (90-95%) 5 x 20 meter "Block" Starts
HURDLERS: 1 x 50 meter "Fly's (90-95%)3 x 1 Hurdle, 2 x 3 hurdles
100 HURDLERS: 1 x 50 meter Fly's (90-95%) 3 x 1 hurdle, 2 x 3H
***400 Meter Relay Hand-off's

Saturday **TRACK MEET**

Sunday
Sprinters & Hurdlers: 15 Minute run   6 x 100's Flexibility Drills

****DO 2-3 Morning Runs of 15-20 minutes & Flex. Drills****

Event Specific Training
(400 Meters, 300 Hurdles & 800 Meters)   Week #10

Monday   Jog 1600-2000 Meters
Dynamic Flex/Hurdle Drills/Sprint Drills/5 x 70 meters
400 METERS: 450 Meters(90%) 200 (85%) 150 (80%)
300 HURDLES: 450 Meters (90%) 200 (85%) 150 (80%)
800 METERS: 5 x 300 Meters (85%)   3-4 min Rest
** WEIGHTS

Tuesday   Jog 1600-2000 Meters
Dynamic Flex/Hurdle Drills/Sprint Drills/5 x 70 meters
400 METERS: 4 x 200 METERS: (85%) 200 Meter Walk
300 HURDLES: 150(70%) 1 x 8 H(85%) 4 x 5 Hurdles (Race Effort)
800 METERS: 20-30 minute Run   8 x 100's "Grass"

Wednesday Jog 20-25 minutes   10 x 100's Strides "GRASS"
Weights

Thursday   Jog 1200-2000 Meters
Dynamic Flex/Hurdle Drills/Sprint Drills/5 x 70 meters
400 METERS: 4 x 100's (70%) Curve's
300 HURDLERS: 2 x 100's (70%) 2 x 1H, 2 x 2 Hurdles, 3 x 3 Hurdles
800 METERS: 5 x 100's (70%) (3 curves & 2 straights)

Friday   Jog 800 -1200 meters
Dynamic Flex/Hurdle Drills/Sprint Drills/5 x 70 meters
400 METERS: 4 x 100   "CURVES FROM BLOCKS HARD-Break Point"
300 HURDLERS: 3 x 1 Hurdle, 2 x 2 hurdles
800 METERS: 6 x 100's "CURVES"& Break Point
###1,600 Relay Hand-Off's X 5

Saturday   **TRACK MEET**

Sunday   Everyone   20-40 minute Run 5 x 100's

**** Do 3-4 Morning Runs of 18-24 Minutes******

Event Specific Training
(Sprints, Hurdles & Relays)   Week #11

Monday
Jog 1200 Meters
Dynamic Flex/Hurdle-Rhythm Drills/Sprint Drills/5 x 70 meters
SPRINTERS: 350 meters (85%)   4 x 50 meter "Fly's" (90-95%)
HURDLERS: 350 meters (85%)   5 x 5 Hurdles (36inches)
100 HURDLERS: 2 x 5 Hurdles Lead/Trail leg, 4 x 8 hurdles
                    (7.5Meters apart) 85-90%
##WEIGHTS##   **** 400 Meter Relay Hand-offs***

Tuesday
Jog 1200 Meters
Dynamic Flex/Hurdle Drills/Sprint Drills/ 5 x 70 meters
SPRINTERS: 5 x 100 Meter-Fly's (90-95%)
HURDLERS:100(70%),300 hurdles 1 x 9H(Sprint Home) 2 x5H, 2 x 2H
****400 Meter Relay Hand-offs***

Wednesday
Jog 1200 Meters
Dynamic Flex/Hurdle Drills/Sprint Drills/ 5 x 70 meters
SPRINTERS: 2 x 250 Meters (85-90%) 5 x 20 meter "Block" Starts
HURDLERS: 1 x 250 Meters (85%) 3 x 10 hurdles (36) 8.5M
100 HURDLERS: 200 Meters (4mR)70-75%
                    4 x 5 Hurdles from blocks (90%)
    ##WEIGHTS##
***400 Meter Relay Hand-off's

Thursday
Jog 1200 Meters
Dynamic Flex Drills/Hurdle Drills/Sprint Drills/ 5 x 70 meters
SPRINTERS: 12 x 100's "GRASS"
HURDLERS: 12 x 100's"GRASS"
*** 400 METER Relay Hand-off's

Friday
Jog 1200 Meters
Dynamic Flex Drills/Hurdle Drills/Sprint Drills/ 5 x 70 meters
SPRINTERS: 2 x 50 meter "Fly's" 95%   5 x 20 meter "Block" Starts
HURDLERS: 1 x 50 meter "Fly's 95%   3 x 1 Hurdle, 2 x 3 hurdles
100 HURDLERS: 1 x 50 meter Fly's 95% 3 x 1 Hurdle, 2 x 3H
***400 Meter Relay Hand-off's

Saturday
TRACK MEET

Sunday
20 minute Jog & Flexibility Drills

Everyone: Do 2-3 Morning Runs of 15-20 minutes & Flexibility Drills

Event Specific Training
(400 Meters, 300 Hurdles & 800 Meters)-Week #11

Monday   Jog 1200-2000 Meters
            Dynamic Flex/Hurdle-Rhythm Drills/Sprint Drills/5 x 70 meters
            400 METERS: 500 Meters (95%),8mR 300 Meters(85%)4mR 200
                    (80%)
            300 HURDLERS: 500 Meters (95%) 8mR 300 Meters (85%)4mR 200
            800 METERS: 1000 Meters (90%) 6mR, 500 Meters (85%)4mR
                    200 (85%) 200(80%)
            ##WEIGHTS#
            400 RELAY HAND-OFFS****

Tuesday   Jog 1200-2000 Meters
            Dynamic Flex/Hurdle-Rhythm Drills/Sprint Drills/5 x 70 meters
            400 METERS: 4 x 250 Meters (85%) 3mR
            300 HURDLES: 100 (70%) 1 x 9 hurdles (Sprint home)=GOAL PACE
                    2 x 5 & 2 x2 hurdles (Race Pace)
            800 METERS: 35-45 Minute Run   "8 x 100's GRASS"

Wednesday   Jog 1200-2000 Meters
            Dynamic Flex/Hurdle-Rhythm Drills/Sprint Drills/5 x 70 meters
            400 METERS: 20 minute run   8 x 100's "Grass"
            300 HURDLES: 20 minute run 10 x 10 hurdles (4 Step R-L)
                    "Training Shoes"
            800 METERS: 600 METERS (95%) 3Mr 4x 200 (75%) 90sR
            ***400 RELAY HAND-OFFS**
            ###WEIGHTS###

Thursday   Jog 1200-2000 Meters
            Dynamic Flex/Hurdle-Rhythm Drills/Sprint Drills/5 x 70 meters
            400 METERS: 3 x 100 Meter "Fly's" (90-95%)
            300 HURDLERS: 3 x 100 Meter "Fly's" (90-95%)
            800 METERS: 30-40 minute Run 6 x 100's "GRASS"
            400 RELAY STICKS

Friday   Jog 1200-2000 METERS
            Dynamic Flex/Hurdle Drills/Sprint Drills/5 x 70Meters
            400 METERS: 5 x 50 meter (Block Starts) "Curve"
            300 HURDLERS: 2 x 1 Hurdle, 2 x 2 Hurdles 1 x 3 hurdles "Blocks"
            800 METERS: 4 x 100 Meters (13) Curves & Straights
            ****EVERYONE 1,600 Meter Relay Hand-off's
            ***400 RELAY STICKS
Saturday   **TRACK MEET**
Sunday   30-40 minute run 5 x100's

*****Everyone Do 2-3 Morning Runs of 18-24 minutes-"EASY"

Event Specific Training
(Sprints, Hurdles & Relays)-Week #12

Monday   Jog 1200 Meters
Dynamic Flex Drills/Hurdle Drills/Sprint Drills/5 x 70 meters
SPRINTERS: 300 Meters (85%)   2x 50,50,50 meters (90-95%)
HURDLERS: 300 Meters (85%)10H,10H,10H,10H (90-95%) "39inch"
100 HURDLERS: 350 Meters (85%) 2 x 5 Lead/Trail Leg
                 5 x 6 hurdles (8.0 meters apart) 90-95%
    ###Weights###

Tuesday   Jog 1200 Meters
Dynamic flex Drills/hurdle Drills/Sprint Drills/5 x 70 meters
SPRINTERS: 5 x 100 Meter "Fly's" (90-95%) 4mR
HURDLERS:300 Hurdles 2 x 8 Hurdles (10 Minute Rest) 3 x 2 hurdles
400 Meter Relay Stick**

Wednesday Jog 1200 meters
Dynamic Flex Drills/Hurdle Drills/Sprint Drills/5 x 70 Meters
SPRINTERS: 12 x 100's 70-75% "Grass" Technique
HURDLERS: 100 (70%) 5 x 5 hurdles (90-95%)
100 HURDLERS: 200 meters (4mR) 70-75% 2 x 5 Lead/Trail leg)
4 x 3 hurdles (7.5 meters apart), 2 x 1 hurdles (7.5 meters apart)
   ###WEIGHTS###
400 Meter Relay Stick

Thursday   Jog 1200 Meters
Dynamic Flex Drills/Hurdle Drills/Sprint Drills/5 x 70 meters
SPRINTERS: 4 x 150 Meters 80-85% "Blocks" Use Full Turn
HURDLERS: 15 minute Run 6 x 100's "GRASS or TURF"
100 HURDLERS: 300 Hurdlers 2 x 1 Hurdles, 2 x 2 Hurdles,
1 x 3 Hurdles from blocks
400 Meter Relay*

FRIDAY   SPRINTERS: 100 (13) 5 x 20 meter "Starts"
HURDLERS: 100 (13) 3 x 1 Hurdle, 2 x 2 hurdles, 1 x 3 hurdles
400 Meter Relay Stick

SATURDAY **TRACK MEET**

Sunday: Jog 15-20 minutes   5 x 100's Flexibility Drills

DEDICATED ATHLETES: Do 2-3 Morning Runs of 15-20 minutes

Event Specific Training
(400 meters, 300 Hurdles & 800 Meters)-Week #12

Monday   Jog 1600-2000 Meters
            Dynamic Flex/Hurdle Drills/Sprint Drills/5 x 70 meters
            400 METERS: 450 Meters (95%)10mR, 1 x 150(85%)
            300 HURDLERS: 450 meters (95%)10mR, 1 x 150(85%)
            800 METERS: 500 Meters (95%)10mR, 500 Meters (85%) 5MR
                           3 x100's (80%)
            ###WEIGHTS###

Tuesday   Jog 1600-2000 Meters
            Dynamic Flex/Hurdle Drills/Sprint Drills/5 x 70 meters
            400 METERS: 2 x 300 Meter (Event Runs) 85% "Sprint-Float-Sprint"
            400 HURDLERS: 150 (19) 2 x 8 hurdles (10 Minute Rest) "Goal Pace"
                          3 x 2 hurdles "Race Effort"
            800 METERS: 25-35 minute Run   8 x 100 Strides "Grass"
            ##400 Relay Stick###

Wednesday   400 METERS: 3 x 150's (Blocks) "Use Full Turn" 85-90%
            400 HURDLERS: 3 x 150's (Blocks) "Use Full Turn" 85-90%
            800 METERS: 300 Meters (80%)4mR 4 x 150's (80%)
            ###WEIGHTS###

Thursday   1600-2000 Meters
            Dynamic Flex/Hurdle Drills/Sprint Drills 5 x 70 meters
            400 METERS: 18-22 Minute Jog 5 x 100's "Grass"
            400 HURDLERS: 18-22 Minute Jog 5 x 100's "Grass"
            800 METERS: 25-30 Minute Run 5 x 100's "Grass"

Friday   Jog 1200-2000 Meters
            Dynamic Flex/Hurdle Drills/Sprint Drills/5 x 70 meters
            400 METERS: 2 x 100 meters (Blocks)
            300 HURDLERS: 3 x 1 Hurdles, 2 x 2 Hurdle 1 x 3 hurdles
            800 METERS: 15 Minute Run   4 x 100's (Straights & Curves)
            ###1,600 Relay Stick

Saturday   **TRACK MEET**

Sunday: 20-30 Minute Run-Easy   5 x 100's   Flex Drills

EVERYONE 2-3 Morning Runs of 15-20 minutes "EASY"

Event Specific Training
(Sprint, Hurdles & Relays)-Week #13

Monday
Jog 1200 Meters
Dynamic Flex/Hurdle Drills/Sprint Drills/ 5 x 70 meters
SPRINTERS: 350 meters (95%) 10mR, From Block 2 x 30,40,50
               (90-95%) 3mR,10mR-sets
HURDLERS: 350 meters (95%) 10mR, 4 x 10 Hurdles"8.5 m"(85-90%)
100 HURDLERS: 5 x 5 lead/trail leg   350 meters (95%) 10mR
               4 x 10 Hurdles (8.0 meters apart) 85-90%
###Weights###

Tuesday
Jog 1200 Meters
Dynamic Flex/Hurdle Drills/Sprint Drills/ 5 x 70 meters
SPRINTERS: 4 x 100 Meter "Fly"   (90-95%)   4mR
HURDLERS:100 (12) 1 x 9 hurdles Sprint=Home "GOAL PACE"
               2 x 3 hurdles (Race Pace)
###400 Meter Relay Stick###

Wednesday   Jog 1200 Meters
Dynamic Flex Drills/hurdle Drills/Sprint Drills/5 x 70 meters
SPRINTERS: 15 Minute Jog   4 x 100's GRASS
HURDLERS: 18 Minute Jog   4 x 100's GRASS
100 HURDLERS: 18 Minute Jog 4 x 100's GRASS
Weights####
****400 METER RELAY STICK

Thursday
Jog 1200 Meters
Dynamic Flex Drills/Hurdle Drills/Sprint Drills/5 x 70 meters
SPRINTERS: 2 x 250 meters (80-85%) 3mR
HURDLERS: 200(70%) 300 Hurdles: 4 x 5 hurdles (80-85%
400 Meter Relay Stick###

Friday
Jog 1200 Meters
Dynamic Flex Drills/Hurdle Drills/Sprint Drills/5 x 70 meters
SPRINTERS:1 x 50 meter "FLY" (95%)   4 x 20 Meter Starts
HURDLERS: 1 x 50 meter "FLY" (95%) HIGHS: 3 x 1 Hurdle
               2 x 2 hurdle (110/300's)
100 HURDLERS: 1 x 50 meter "FLY" 3 x 1 hurdle, 2 x 2 hurdles

###1,600 Relay Stick####

Saturday   **Track Meet**

Sunday   20 Minute Run 6 x 100's grass Flexibility Drills

SERIOUS ATHLETES: 2-3 Morning Runs 15-18 minutes

Event Specific Training
(400 METERS, 300 HURDLERS & 800 Meters)-Week #13

Monday   Jog 1600-2000 METERS
            Dynamic Flex Drills/Hurdle Drills/Sprint Drills/5 x 70 meters
            400 METERS: 500 Meters (95%) 10mR, 3 x 200 Meters (75%)
            300 HURDLERS: 500 Meters (95%) 10mR, 3 x 200 Meters (75%)
            800 METERS: 1000Meters(95%)10mR,500 Meters 85% 2 x 200 (75%)
            ###WEIGHTS###

Tuesday   Jog 1600-2000 Meters
            Dynamic Flex/Hurdle Drills/Sprint Drills/5 x 70 meters
            400 METERS: 5 x 100 Meter "Fly's"   (90-95%)
            300 HURDLERS: (100)70% 1 x 9 hurdles Sprint Home=GOAL PACE
                          2 x 3 Hurdles (race pace)
            800 METERS: 25-30 Minute run 5 x 100 Strides   "GRASS"
            ##400 Meter Relay Hand-offs

Wednesday   Jog 1600-2000 Meters
            Dynamic Flex Drills/Hurdle Drills/Sprint Drills/5 x 70 meters
            400 METERS: 20-25 minute Jog 8 x 100's "GRASS"
            300 HURDLERS: 20-25 Minute Run 8 x 100's "GRASS"
            800 METERS: 5 x 200's (Race Pace) 3mR
            ###WEIGHTS###
            ###400 Meter Relay Hand-offs

Thursday   Jog 1600-2000 Meters
            Dynamic Flex/hurdle Drills/Sprint Drills/5 x 70 meters
            400 METERS: 4 x 150 meters (85%)
            300 HURDLERS: 200 (75%) 5 x 5 hurdles (RACE PACE)
            800 METERS: 20-30 minute run   5 x100 Strides
            #400 METER RELAY HAND-OFFS

Friday   Jog 1200-2000 Meters
            Dynamic Flex/Hurdle Drills/Sprint Drills/5 x 70 meters
            400 METERS: 3 x 100 meters (Blocks)
            300 HURDLERS:3 x 1 Hurdles, 2 x 2 Hurdle, 1 x 3 hurdles (Race Pace)
            800 METERS: 15 Minute Run   4 x 100's (Straights & Curves)
            ###1,600 Relay Stick

Saturday   **TRACK MEET**

Sunday   30-55 Minute Run –Easy

            Everyone: 2-3 MORNING Run 15-20 minutes-EASY

Event Specific Training
(Sprints, Hurdles & Relays)   Week #14

Monday   Jog 1200 Meters
              Dynamic Flex Drills/Hurdle Drills/Sprint Drills/5 x 70 meters
              SPRINTERS:300 METERS(95%)10mR 2 (50,50,50) Blocks 90-95%
                      3mR 10mR-sets
              HURDLERS:300 METERS (95%) 10mR 3(10H,10H,10H,) 39 inches
              90-95%
              100 HURDLERS: 300METERS (95%)3 x (10H,10H,10H) normal 95%
              ####WEIGHT ROOM####
              ***400 Meter Relay Hand-off's

Tuesday   Jog 1200 Meters
              Dynamic Flex Drills/Hurdle Drills/Sprint Drills/5 x 70 meters
              SPRINTERS: 2 x 250 Meters (85%)
              HURDLERS: 100 (70%) 300 Hurdles:1 x 8 Hurdles, 2 x 5 hurdles,
                      1 x 3 Hurdles (RACE PACE)
              ***400 Meter Hand-off's

Wednesday Jog 1200 Meters
              Dynamic Flex/Hurdle Drills/Sprint Drills/5 x 70 meters
              SPRINTERS: 3 x 100 Meter "Fly's" (90-95%) 5mR
              HURDLERS: 18 minute "Jog"   5 x 100's GRASS
              ###WEIGHT ROOM###
              ***400 Meter Relay Hand-off's

Thursday   Jog 1200 Meters
              Dynamic Flex Drills/Hurdle Drills/Sprint Drills/5 x 70 meters
              SPRINTERS: 10 x 100's (70-75%) Grass "Technique"
              HURDLERS: 100 "Fly's (90-95%) 300 Hurdles: 4 x 5 H from Blocks
              100 HURDLERS: 100 Fly (90-95%) 300 Hurdles: 4 x 5 H from Blocks
               ***400 Meter Relay Hand-off's

Friday   Pre-Meet Shakeout
              SPRINTERS:1 x 50 Meter "Fly" 90-95%, 4 x 20 meters (Blocks)
              HURDLERS: 1 x 50 Meter "Fly" 90-95%, 3 x 1 Hurdle, 2 x 2 Hurdles
              100 HURDLERS: 1 x 50 Meter "Fly" 90-95% 3 x 1 Hurdle, 2 x 2 H
               ###400 Meter Relay###

SATURDAY   **TRACK MEET**

Sunday   12-20 Minute Jog   "Flexibility Drills"

SERIOUS ATHLETES: 2-3 Morning Jog 10-15 Minutes & Flexibility Drills

Event Specific Training
(300 Hurdles, 400 Meters, 800 Meters)-Week #14

Monday   Jog 1600-2000 Meters
Dynamic Flex/Hurdle Drills/Sprint Drills/5 x 70 meters (Hard)
400 METERS: 450 Meters (95%10mR, 250 meters (85-90%)6mR,
                  100 Fly (90%)
300 HURDLERS: 450 Meters (95%)10mR,250 meters (85-90%)6mR
                  100 Fly (90%)
800 METERS: 600 Meters (9%%) 10mR 3 x 100's (70-75%)
###WEIGHT ROOM###

Tuesday   Jog 1600-2000 Meters
Dynamic Flex/Hurdle Drills/Sprint Drills/5 x 70 meters (Hard)
400 METERS: 20 minute Run   6 x 100 Strides
300 HURDLERS: 100 (75%) 1 x 8 Hurdles (90%), 2 x 5 Hurdles,
                1 x 3 Hurdles (RACE PACE)
800 METERS: 25-30 Minute Run   8 x 100's "GRASS"

Wednesday Jog 1600-2000 Meters
Dynamic Flex/Hurdle Drills/Sprint Drills/5 x 70 meters (Hard)
400 METERS: 4 x 100 Meter "Flys" 5mR (90-95%)
300 HURDLERS: 20 Minute Run 6 x 100's Strides GRASS
800 METERS: 2 x 300 meters (70-75%)   2 x 100 "Fly's" (90-95%)
###WEIGHT ROOM###

Thursday   Jog 1600-2000 Meters
Dynamic Flex/Hurdle Drills/Sprint Drills/5 x 70 meters (Hard)
400 METERS: 18 minute Run   8 x 100's "Grass"
300 HURDLERS:150m(75%),2 x 5 Hurdles, 1 x 3 hurdles (Race Pace)
800 METERS: 20-25 Minute Run   6 x 100's "Grass"

Friday   Jog 1200-2000 Meters
Dynamic Flex/Hurdle Drills/Sprint Drills/5 x 70 meters (Hard)
400 METERS: 3 x 100's (75%) "Curve"   1,600 Relay Hand-off's
300 HURDLERS: 2 x 1 Hurdle, 2 x 2 Hurdles 1,600 Relay Hand-off's
800 METERS: 4 x 100's(12-13)"Curves"   1,600 Relay Hand-off's

Saturday   **TRACK MEET**

Sunday   20-30 Minute Run "Easy"

Do 2 Morning Runs of 18-25 minutes####

Event Specific Training
(Sprints/Hurdles/Relays)-Week #15

CHAMPIONSHIP CYCLE

Monday   Jog 1200 Meters
Dynamic Flex/Hurdle Drills/Sprint Drills/ 5 x 70 Meters
SPRINTERS: 250 Meters 85% 8mR, 3 x 50 meters (90-95%)3mR
HURDLERS: 250 Meters-85% 8mR, 3 x 10 High Hurdles (36)
       "Goal Pace" 8mR
100 HURDLERS 250 (85%) 8mR   3 x 10Hurdles "Goal Pace" 8mR
WEIGHT ROOM###
400 METER RELAY STICK

Tuesday   Jog 1200 Meters
Dynamic Flex/Hurdle Drills/Sprint Drills/5 x 70 meter Strides
SPRINTERS: 400 Meter Relay Stick Only   5 x 20 starts
HURDLERS: 100 (75%) 300 Hurdles, 2 x 8 Int. Hurdles (85%) 10mR
400 METER RELAY STICK

Wednesday Jog 1200 Meters
Dynamic Flex/Hurdle Drills/Sprint Drills/5 x 70 meters
SPRINTERS: 2 x 150 Meter "Fly's" 90-95%   4 x 20 meter Starts
HURDLERS: 150 (75%) 2 x 10hurdles (36 inches) 90-95% 4 x 1H
(Race Pace)
100 HURDLERS: 150 (75%) 2 x 10 hurdles 90-95% 3 x 1 Hurdle
(Race Pace)
###WEIGHT ROOM####

Thursday   Jog 1200 Meters
Dynamic Flex/Hurdle Drills/Sprint Drills/5 x 70 meters
SPRINTERS: 3 x 100 Meter "Fly's" (90-95%)
HURDLERS: 3 x 100 Meter "Fly's" (90-95%)
***400 METER RELAY STICK

Friday   Jog 1200 Meters
Dynamic Flex Drills/Hurdle Drills/Sprint Drills/5 x 70 meters
SPRINTERS: 8 x 100 Meters   "Grass"
HURDLERS: 8 x 100 Meters   "Grass"
100 HURDLERS: 8 x 100 Meters   "Grass"

Saturday   Jog 1200 Meters
Dynamic Flex/Hurdle Drills/Sprint Drills/5 x 70 meters
SPRINTERS: 300 "(Fly" (90-95%)15mR 200 "Fly" (90-95%)10mR
      100 (Fly)
HURDLERS: (10H)10mR (10H)10mR,(10H)(36 inches)"FAST"(95%)

Sunday   Everyone 15-20 minute Grass Jog!

Event Specific Training
(400 Meters, 300 Hurdles, 800 Meters)-Week #15

<u>**"CHAMPIONSHIP CYCLE"**</u>

Monday   Jog 1600-2000 Meters
                 Dynamic Flex Drills/Hurdle Drills/Sprint Drills/5 x 70 meters
                 400 METERS: 500 Meters (95%)   2 x 150 meters (85%)
                 300 HURDLERS: 500 Meters (95%)   2 x 150 meters (85%)
                 800 METERS: 1200 Meters (95%) 8mR 500 (85%)& Kick Hard (4mR)
                         Race Pace then Kick Hard!!!!
                 ###WEIGHT ROOM###   **1,600 Relay Hand-off's***

Tuesday   Jog 1600-2000 Meters
                 Dynamic Flex Drills/Hurdle Drills/Sprint Drills/5 x 70 meters
                 400 METERS: 20-25 Minute Run, 6 x 100 strides
                 300 HURDLERS: 20-25 Minute Run, 6 x 100 strides
                 800 METERS: 30-35 Minute Run, 6 x 100 strides

Wednesday Jog 1600-2000 Meters
                 Dynamic Flex Drills/Hurdle Drills/Sprint Drills/5 x 70 meters
                 400 METERS: 4 x 100 Meter Fly's   (90-95%)
                 300 HURDLERS: 100 (12) 2 x 8 hurdles (85%) "RACE PACE" 10mR
                 800 METERS: 700 meters (95%)"Goal Pace"10mR, 2 x 200(75%) 2MR
                 ###WEIGHT ROOM##

Thursday   Jog 1600-2000 Meters
                 Dynamic Flex Drills/Hurdle Drills/Sprint Drills/5 x 70 meters
                 400 METERS: 4 x 200's "Race Pace" with 5min Rest @
                 300 HURDLERS: 4 x 200's "Race Pace" with 5 min Rest
                 800 METERS: 6 x 200 meters Race Pace" 2mR "RELAXED"
                 1,600 Relay Hand-off's

Friday   Jog 1600-2000 Meters
                 Dynamic Flex Drills/Hurdle Drills/Sprint Drills/5x 70 meters
                 400 METERS: 20-25 Minute Run, 6 x 100 strides
                 300 HURDLERS: 20-25 Minute Run, 6 x 100 strides
                 800 METERS: 25-35 Minute Run, 6 x 100 strides
                  ####WEIGHTS####

Saturday   **MANDATORY TEAM WORKOUT**
                 400 METERS: 300 "FLY"(95%)15mR 200 "Fly"(95%)100 "Fly" 95%
                 300 HURDLERS: 300"FLY"(95%)15mR 200 "Fly" (95%)100"Fly"-95%
                 800 METERS: 3 x 400 Meters (90-95%) "Goal Pace" 5mR

Sunday   15-25 minute grass jog!
                 ## Morning Runs of 15-20 minutes just two days#

"CHAMPIONSHIP CYCLE"

Monday   Jog 1200 Meters
            Dynamic Flex Drills/Hurdle Drills/Sprint Drills/5 x 70 meters
            SPRINTERS: 15 minute run   6 x 100's (85%) "grass"
            HURDLERS: 15 minute run   6 x 100's "(85%) grass"
            100 HURDLES: 15 minute run   6 x 100's "(85%) grass"
            *** WEIGHT ROOM******
            ##400 Meter Relay Hand-Offs###

Tuesday   Jog 1200 Meters
            Dynamic Flex/Hurdle Drills/Sprint Drills/5 x 70 meters
            SPRINTERS: 2-3 x 50 Meter "FLYS" (90-95%) 4 x 20m Block Starts
            HURDLERS: 300 Hurdles: 1 x 9 hurdles and Sprint Home="Goal pace"
                      2 x 2 hurdles "Goal Pace"
            ###400 Meter Relay Hand-off's

Wednesday   Jog 1200 Meters
            Dynamic Flex/Hurdle Drills/Sprint Drills/5 x 70 meters
            SPRINTERS: 200 (75%) 5 x 20 meters (Blocks)
            HURDLERS: 100 (75%) 2 x 5 hurdles   3 x 1 hurdles (Race Pace)
            100 HURDLERS: 100 (75%) 2 x 5 hurdles, 3 x 1 hurdles (Race Pace)
            ###400 Meter Relay Hand-off's####

Thursday   Jog 1200 Meters
            Dynamic Flex/Hurdle Drills/Sprint Drills/5 x 70 meters
            SPRINTERS: 6 x 100 meters "Grass" Strides
            HURDLERS: 6 x 100 meters "Grass" Strides

Friday   Jog 1200 METERS
            Dynamic Flex/Hurdle Drills/Sprint Drills/5 x 70 meters
            SPRINTERS: 100 (75%)   4 x 20 meter "Block" Starts
            HURDLERS: 100 (75%)   3 x 1 Hurdle & 2 x 2 Hurdles (Race Pace)
            100 HURDLERS 100 (75%) 3 x 1 Hurdle & 2 x Hurdles (Race Pace)
            ##400 Meter Relay Hand-off's##

Saturday   **STATE OR NATIONAL MEET   "Kick Ass & Take Names"**

No Morning Runs this week!

CHAMPIONSHIP CYCLE"

Monday   Jog 1600-2000 Meters
Dynamic Flex/Hurdle Drills/Sprint Drills/5 x 70 meters
400 METERS: 18-20 minute Run   4 x 100's "Grass"
300 HURDLES: 18-20 minute Run   4 x 100's "Grass"
800 METERS: 25-30 Minute Run 4 x 100's "Grass"
###WEIGHT ROOM###

Tuesday   Jog 1600-2000 Meters
Dynamic Flex/Hurdle Drills/Sprint Drills/ 5 x 70 meters
400 METERS: 3 x 200 meters (90%)
300 HURDLERS: 1 x 9 Hurdles & SPRINT HOME=GOAL PACE,
                  2 x 2 hurdles "Race Pace"
800 METERS: 2 x 300 meters 70-75% 3mR, 2 x 100 "Flys" 90-95%
###1,600 Meter Sticks###

Wednesday Jog 1600-2000 Meters
Dynamic Flex/Hurdle Drills/Sprint Drills/5 x 70 meters
400 METERS: 2-3 x 100 Meter Flys (90-95%)
300 HURDLERS: 2-3 x 100 Meter Fly's (90-95%)
800 METERS: 20 minute run   4 x 100s "Curves"
##1,600 Meter Sticks###

Thursday   400 METERS: 18-20 minutes, 5 x 100's "GRASS"
400 HURDLERS: 15-20 minutes, 5 x 100's "GRASS"
800 METERS: 20-30 minutes, 5 x 100's "GRASS"

Friday   1600-2000 METERS
Dynamic Flex/Hurdle Drills/Sprint Drills 5 x 70 Meters
400 METERS: 3 x 100's Curves, 4 x 20 meters "Blocks Starts"
400 HURDLERS: 2 x 1 Hurdles, 2 x 2 hurdles, 1 x 3 hurdles (R PACE)
800 METERS: 4 x 100 Meters "Curves " 90-95%
##1,600 Meter Sticks##

Saturday   **STATE or NATIONAL MEET "Kick Ass and Take Names"**

Sunday   REST

Only 1-2 Morning Runs this week!

IMPORTANT COACHING INFORMATION CONCERNING TRACK & FIELD

Cutting-Edge Preparation for Track & Field
By
Coach Steve Silvey
Championship SSE Products
Dallas, Texas

As many of you are aware, you practice the sport of track and field for 1-2 hours a day. However, what you may not know is that the remaining 22 hours a day is the MOST critical to your success.

You can be a World Class Athlete at practice doing all of the right things, but what you do the other 22 hours of the day dictates how average, good or great you will be. You are on your own during those 22 hours. To be GREAT you must:

1. **HYDRATE PROPERLY** – 100+ ounces of preferably water but Sport Drinks and juices count. Carbonated drinks DO NOT count. If you do not have to go to the bathroom every hour then you are not properly hydrated!!!!!! Pedialyte is one of the best items on the market for providing high levels of electrolytes.

2. **NUTRITION** - 3 well rounded meals per day that include fruits and vegetables for important nutrients and minerals that enable the body to function. 24 hours prior to a competition it is to your benefit to consume Complex Carbohydrates such as pasta, rice, potatoes breads and pancakes. Eat protein early in the week to help repair muscle tissue that is damaged by intense training. STAY AWAY from desserts 48 hours prior to a competition as the refined sugar contained in desserts can turn off fast twitch muscle firing. MINIMIZE "fast foods" which contain very little nutritional value and large amounts of fat.

3. **SLEEP** - 7-8 hours at night that begins before midnight. Sleep is probably the most common area neglected by college athletes but is one of the most important to address. Athletes who do not get enough rest are prone to injuries. Over-sleeping is just as bad as not getting enough sleep. Sleeping 9-12 hours makes the body sluggish and affects the quality of the workout and performance at competitions.

4. **AVOID CAFFEINE & ALCOHOL** – Caffeine is a natural diuretic which means it causes you to lose water stored in your body. Caffeine and alcohol deplete the body of "B" vitamins and can have an adverse affect on many other parts of your body. When you lose the water in your system you are more likely to become dehydrated because you will not have the

stores in your system for your body to use. When the 'B' vitamin levels are depleted then you are more prone to illness and athletic injuries. Caffeine is found in carbonated drinks, tea and coffee.

5. **AVOID AFTERNOON NAPS** - Studies have shown that when you take a nap 1-2 hours prior to a workout or competition it causes the body's fast twitch muscle fibers to become sluggish. First of all whenever possible GET PLENTY OF GOOD SLEEP so you don't need to nap. Then if you are feeling tired get up and out to eliminate the desire to sleep.

6. **MONITOR YOUR BODY WEIGHT** – What did you weigh when you ran your lifetime best? Well, where are you today? To find out your ideal weight, ask the trainers or coaches help you to determine what your ideal body weight should be for your sport. It is common to gain weight in college because you have the freedom to choose what goes into your mouth. It's easy to gain 10 pounds and not notice it, but it shows in your athletic performance. If you don't believe it try this exercise. Fill a backpack with 10 pounds of books or whatever you wish. Do your workout with the backpack on your back and see how you feel. If you have gained 2, 3, or 10 pounds it came on gradually and you probably didn't notice it. By adding 10 pounds suddenly you notice the effect it has on your performance level. Guess what? The effect is the same whether it comes on gradually or suddenly. To be at your best you have to maintain the optimum weight for your body performing in your event. Keep in mind that even 2 – 5 pounds over your ideal weight can put a lot of strain on your muscles especially your hamstrings with the end result being an athletic injury.

7. **DAILEY MORNING EXERCISE** – A morning jog with stretching for about 10-15 minutes will make you more alert in class and better in your afternoon workout.

8. **WARM-UP FOR SECOND EVENT**- Athletes must learn to properly warm-up for their second event. This warm-up does not Have to be as long as that for the first event but needs to be done for at least 15-20 minutes. 5 hard strides need to be done prior to the start of the athlete's next event.

9 **WARMING-UP FOR A THIRD EVENT**-Once again the athlete must warm-up 15-20 minutes for their third event. 5 fast strides prior to the event will ensure that the athlete is ready to perform at their best!

10 **FLEXIBILITY**-Great athletes will spend extra time to work on their flexibility. This means devoting additional time away from the afternoon practice to ADD more flexibility. This can be done in the shower at home, later in the evening or in the morning after a light jog. This extra time will help the athletes to reduce injuries. I am a firm believer that the hurdler must be the most flexible athlete on the entire track team. I suggest you invest in a *Stretch-Rite belt*. This device allows the athletes to do stretching that normally requires a second person to help with. Partner stretching can often hurt your star athletes by someone not paying attention and "overstretching" them. *This Stretch-Rite belt* can be found at: *SSEproducts.com*

11 **DEDICATION TO THE SPORT**-Great Athlete must become a student of their event! I am a firm believer in the following statement that I came up with while coaching at the University of Oregon.

"PART-TIME ATHLETES GET PART-TIME RESULTS"

The bottom line is that YOU choose how good you want to be in the sport of track and field. Elite athletes must make many sacrifices that most students-athletes do not. Athletes who lack self-discipline for these 22 hours of the day are only fooling themselves. Self-discipline is a very important quality that will make you successful the rest of your life. The choice is yours!

SUPER NUTRITION FOR THE HIGH LEVEL ATHLETE
By
Coach Steve Silvey
Championship SSE Products
SSEproducts.com

Athletes are becoming more and more interested in how diet affects their athletic performance. It is now recognized that the right diet, combined with the latest nutritional supplements and combined with proper training and coaching can significantly improve the overall performance of today's athlete.

I have stated to my athletes many times that you can be the greatest trained athlete in the world, but with poor eating habits, he or she will be no better than the athlete who trains only half as hard yet employs a good well-rounded nutritional program. Athletes must also get their proper sleep at night!

I have noticed many athletes trying to consume a fast-food meal hours before a competition or between prelims and finals of a same day competition, only to learn that their choice of food usually comes with a large percentage of fat (25-39 grams). This meal did little to aid in their athletic performance. Most importantly these Athletes often complain of little energy, feeling sick with side aches or nausea. When will today's athletes and coaches wise up?

I suggest that the coach or athlete pack a small sack lunch to be eaten hours before competition or between matches, which consists of the following:

- Orange

- Banana

- Apple

- Pretzels or crackers

- Granola or energy bar

- Chicken or turkey sandwich

- Non-carbonated drink

On the day of the competition the athletes should not consume any sweets if possible, as they will often slow down or shut off the body's energy flow. Only consume foods that are naturally sweet such as fruits. An example of this sacrifice is Andre Cason, the 1993 Silver Medalist in the World Track and Field Championships for the 100 meters (9.93) Cason had a strong desire for ice cream but would make it a firm decline of the product within 48 hours leading up to the race.

Athletes should also stay away from greasy, fried, fatty foods and red meats before competition, Try to load up on complex carbohydrates such as pasta and pizza the night before the competition. These are quick energy foods that help you sustain energy for several hours.

Athletes should also be consuming vast quantities of fruits and vegetables in their diet, at least two meals a day. Hydration is very important to the success of the athlete. I ask you, would your car work if you did not put gas and oil in it? The same holds true for your body, as you must consume 8-12 glasses of fluid on a daily basis. This would mean 100 ounces of fluid a day! I am a firm believer that if the athlete does not have to use the restroom every hour, they are not hydrated properly. Athletes should also limit the amount of carbonated drinks that they consume. Sports Drinks contain lots of sugars which are not good for an athlete. I have found that the best item is **Pedialyte.** This product contains more electrolytes than any other product on the market. This is what they give to young babies to prevent dehydration!

What is a healthy diet? Nearly all of the foods and drinks that we consume contain varying quantities of different nutrients and provide us with energy.

We must also not forget the four basic food groups:

1) Milk Group

2) Meat Group

3) Vegetables & Fruits

4) Breads & Cereals

Junk food manuafactures bombard our athletes with millions of dollars' worth of advertisements, extolling the benefits of their products, we as coaches find ourselves waging a constant battle without athletes over their eating habits.

The bottom line: junk foods are easily accessible and have a strong appeal to the young athlete. But there are alternatives. As coaches we can help guide the young athlete and help him or her eat properly by providing them with a greater knowledge of what is correct nutrition and also providing that information to their parents.

Today's athletes need 3000 calories a day. Many people today in this fast society of ours don't understand correct caloric intake. Most people in our society consume many more calories of protein and fats than are recommended in a nutritious diet. For the athlete, this is even a bigger problem, because athletes preparing for a big competition must stay lean! Over eating is a big problem in our society.

Stay away from these so called energy drinks as they contain extremely high levels of caffeine or illegal supplements. These can lead to dehydration or produce a very high heart rate that could lead to death!

I am a firm believer in "legal" nutritional supplements to aid the athlete in their quest to maximize their athletic abilities.

Some of these items are as follows:

Multiple Vitamins

Phosphate Supplement

Calcium/Magnesium Supplement (Osteo-Tech)

Fruit/Vegetable Supplement

Protein Supplement (Creatine)

Vitamin D-3

I have been using **Phosphates (*Phosphate Plus*)** with my athletes for almost 20 years. They help in reducing muscle cramps, strains, pulls and lactic acid build-up from intense workouts. This is the equivalent to eating 8-9 bananas a day!

I also suggest a calcium/magnesium supplement **(*Osteo-Tech*)** help's the athletes with natural muscle contraction, reduces stress fractures and aids in speeding up athletic injuries such as hamstring strains or pulls.

A fruit and vegetable supplement **(*Fruit & Veggie Power*)** can insure the athlete's gets enough fruits and vegetables in their daily diet.

As long as the young athlete does a great job of consuming 8-10 glasses of water a day, creatine **(*C-Power Sports Creatine*)** is still a great product to help them improve strength levels in young athletes that needs to get stronger. Again these legal supplements may be found on my website: SSEproducts.com.

With regards to *(**Vitamin D-3**)* please go to the top left side of my website **SSEproducts.com** to read an awesome 10 page research article written by a leading medical researcher. Vitamin D-3 is often referred to as the sunshine vitamin. This product is helpful to the athlete in some many positive ways!

I have seen some amazing developments in the training and performance of my athletes since I have begun using some of these "legal" nutrition supplements. From a track and field standpoint, the U.S.A. Olympic Committee has an illegal drug list of more than 150 banned substances. If an athlete takes one by mistake, they could be banned for a period of 1-4 years by the NCAA or the U.S.A. Olympic Committee or other governing associations.

Many of these suspensions happen because they walk into a sports nutrition store and are told to buy several products that have banned substances in them. So be careful and read the labels!

For further information about these products go to my website:

SSE products.com

<u>Important Nutritional Guidelines</u>

➢ Eat chicken or fish as often for your meat choice.

➢ Carbohydrates such as pasta or pizza are great pre-competition meals.

➢ Keep a majority of fruits and vegetables in your diet. They are low in fat and calories. They contain important vitamins and nutrients that your body needs to function.

➢ Eat Something "GREEN" at lunch or dinner.

➢ Try to avoid carbonated drinks whenever possible.

➢ Consume 8-10 glasses of water each day to stay properly hydrated.

➢ Try to eat one or two bananas each morning at breakfast.

➢ When you must have something sweet, have an orange, apple, pear, etc. or even some yogurt.

➢ Stay away from energy drinks.

➢ A great athlete must keep an eye on their body weight and must think of their bodies nutritional needs.

➢ Today's athletes should be knowledgeable of the latest products on the market. Some of these can legally aid in recovery, handling stress and most importantly, performance.

To be a champion, you must always get your rest, and eat the proper foods necessary to fuel your body!

PRE-RACE MEAL SUGGESTIONS

by
Coach Steve Silvey
Championship SSE Products

Dinner (Night Before)

- Some Type of Pasta (Spaghetti, Lasagna or Non-greasy Pizza)
- Salad
- Vegetables
- Garlic Bread
- Non-Carbonated Drink or Water
- Banana, Orange or Apple

Stay away from Deserts that have lots of sugars. Large doses of sugar will turn off the athlete's muscle receptors. This will make you feel weak & sluggish the next day.

Breakfast (3-4 hours before race)

- Orange Juice
- Pancakes, Waffles, French Toast, Toast with Honey or Jelly
- Granola Bar
- Banana
- Orange or Apple
- Water

Stay away from milk 4-5 hours before a race! The athlete should feel hungry before lining up for their race.

Hydration

Hydration starts 24 hours before the race. By consuming 100 ounces of fluid over a 24 hour period that athlete will be properly hydrated. If the athlete does not have to go to the bathroom every hour, they are not properly hydrated. For muscle to work at 100%, they must be hydrate. ***Proper Hydration = Maximizing Athletic Performance***

Vitamins

Athletes should take a good multiple vitamins each morning with their breakfast. Vitamins and minerals are often needed to cope with the rigors of training and racing. If the athlete doe not need it, they will merely pass it out of their system when going to the bathroom.

Sleep

Since most athletes are nervous the night before the meet the most critical night for sleep is two nights before. If you race on Saturday, then this would be Thursday night.

THE
HURDLES

Coaching The Women's 100 Meter Hurdles

By
Steve Silvey
The University of Arkansas

Hurdling in the sport of track and field has changed from the old concept of jumping the hurdle to spiting over the barriers. The physical development of today's athletes has come through systematic training and improvement of track surfaces and equipment, thus making these athletes better suited to sprinting over these barriers.

The Women 100 meter hurdles event must be thought of as a sprinting event. Acceleration as well as maintenance of high velocity throughout the race is the key elements of success. In analyzing world class hurdlers, it has been shown that acceleration does not stop at the first hurdle, but rather continues through the 4th and 5th hurdle. It shall be noted that the 100 meter hurdlers accelerate approximately for the same distance before reaching top velocity. Also the stabilization of maximum velocity is extremely high though hurdles 6, 7, 8, and 9. Speed endurance or more specifically, rhythm endurance is well developed by successful hurdlers.

From the start to the first hurdle, the hurdler should us an eight stride pattern. The rhythm used in running these eight strides to the first hurdle is much closer to the rhythm used between the remainder of the hurdles and thus helps the athlete get into their rhythm sooner.

It is very important that the hurdler attack the first 4-5 strides with a similar inclination of the body found in the normal acceleration from the starting blocks.

Once she is within the last three strides before the hurdle, she should position to attack the hurdle in a more upright position to attack the hurdle in a more effective posture for proper hurdle clearance. Remember, the first five strides should be driving and powerful with strides 6-8 emphasizing an increase in cadence much as in the rhythm of the inter-hurdle run.

The 100 meter hurdle should pay close attention to the trail leg. This foot will be the one she uses to propel herself into the hurdle. We will not use the term "take-off foot" because too many athletes associate this tem with jumping! The trail leg will initiate longer strides than those initiated by the lead foot.

One concept I feel is often overlooked is the Cut-step. The stride before the hurdle is slightly shorter than the previous stride and involves a lighter, active landing action of the power foot to keep the projection of the center of mass over the hurdle low and well directed. By using an active landing, the hurdler will have a very quick placing of the trail leg in the power position than in the previous stride. Also, using this active landing prior to the hurdle, will help the ""cut" or shorten the last stride and minimize loss of velocity going into the hurdle. This placement should be on the toes and occurs approximately 2 meters from the hurdle.

The lead leg action is very important factor that controls hurdle clearance. Once the hurdlers led leg finishes it propulsive phase before the hurdle, it immediately is recovered, heel to butt, as the knee is driven up at the point over the hurdle. This requires flexion at the knee and hip. The lower leg remains tucked under the lead leg thigh until the thigh is parallel to the ground. When the hurdlers thigh has reached the apex, momentum is then transferred to the lower leg by extending the knee joint.

The knee does not lock! Too many young hurdles try to cheat and lock the lead leg. That ends up being a longer lever and a slower leaver! Another reason for hip flexion and lower leg extension is that the rectus femoris and hamstring muscles are multiple jointed muscles which cross over the hip and knee. A characteristic of such muscles is they do not permit complete movement in both joints simultaneously.

Once the trial leg loses contact with the ground, the trail leg action will begin once the heel is pulled tight to the butt. The hurdlers knee is then pulled through so it will deviate as little as possible from the mid-line of the body. The knee is also pulled though so it always higher than the ankle. The hurdlers foot is also turned outward by rotating the lower leg externally as well as well as averting at the ankle.

The lead arm action for the hurdle should be one that opposes the lead leg. The arm flexes the shoulder joint forward is a slightly exaggerated manner to balance the lead leg. Once the hurdler passes the hurdle, the lead arm extends forcefully from the shoulder to balance the recovery of the trail leg.

The hurdlers free arm on the same side as the lead leg should deviate as little as possible from the normal sprint form. The elbow remains bent and drives backward on attack to the hurdle and immediately forward as the body passes the hurdle. The hurdlers' trunk should remain tall and more erect than that of the male hurdler and her eyes should be focused up and to the front.

The length of the hurdle stride for the female hurdler which is from take-off to touch-down, should be about 9-10 feet. The lower the hurdle, the less distance should be realized after the hurdle. The hurdle stride should be distributed so that 60% of the distance is accounted for before the hurdle and 40% after the hurdle.

On landing, the lead leg should be actively extended from the hip so the point of contact is virtually below the center of gravity of the hurdler. The knee of the hurdler is slightly flexed, not locked.

As the trail leg makes contact with the ground, the trail leg knee is high and has already been pulled through as much as possible in preparation for the next force application.

The hurdlers getaway stride should consist of the trail leg extending forcefully from the hip so the foot lands under the center of gravity. The leg does not extend at the knee and reaches forward. Because of this inefficient position of the lead leg to apply force off the hurdle, the getaway stride is the shortest stride.

The hurdlers second stride should be the longest stride in the pattern because of the extension of the trail leg. The hips will still remain in a "Hips Tall" position in order to set up the third stride which is the crucial stride in hurdle clearance.

The hurdlers third stride is set up by the forceful drive of the lead leg before the hurdle. The step onto the trail leg should be slightly shorter but very active and high on the balls of the feet. This facilitates forward rotation at take-off. The hurdler should continue to think about keeping the hips tall and avoid over striding our bounding. The key is to sprint between the hurdles! As the hurdle approaches the final hurdle they must still keep the head and eyes up at all times. This is called "Neutral Head Position". This is a common mistake that most young hurdlers make. Failure to properly do this will result in the hurdler crashing and burning on the final hurdle.

As the hurdle begins the run-in from the last hurdle, she should focus on the last phase of the race as this is often neglected. She should know the number of strides from the last hurdle to the finish line so a dip to the tape can be made. It would be a great idea to practice accelerating and driving off the last hurdle to the finish line.

I strongly urge you to look at my "NEW" hurdle book for many drills to improve hurdle speed. These can be found in my second edition of my World Class "Elite" Hurdle Training Program (Book & DVD). This new book is written in a popular "Cookbook" form.

The book has many workouts written for numerous weeks of the season. This book also comes with a DVD that demonstrates various hurdle drills. This book and DVD "package" can be found on my website: **SSEproducts.com or** by calling (972) 294-5696

Good luck in quest of producing many great hurdlers!

Overcoming the Common Hurdling Errors
by
Steve Silvey
Assistant Track Coach
University of Arkansas
NCAA Champions

Hurdling is one of the most beautiful and challenging events in the sport of track and field. Hurdling requires that the athlete develop or have a unique skill-set - rhythm, coordination, grace and extreme flexibility in addition to speed, power, strength, and athleticism.

HURDLING STATE OF MIND
For a hurdler to enter the world of the "elite" athlete, he/she will need to have the right state of mind. A highly aggressive nature and the "mind set" of a western "Gunslinger" are characteristics that can benefit the hurdler. He/she will need the toughness and tenacity of a NFL of a linebacker and like the **"Ninja Warrior"** attack hurdles with **"No Fear"**.

FLEXIBILITY & THE HURDLER
A great hurdler must spend a lot of time on flexibility. The hurdler is one of the most flexible athletes on a track and field team. Flexibility is so important that I consider it a waste of time to work with hurdlers who are not willing to work on improving their flexibility. Good flexibility decreases the following:

1. Technical errors in hurdling
2. Unwanted contact with the hurdle
3. Balance problems
4. Get to the ground quicker
5. Physical injuries

Working on flexibility means that the athlete must devote another 15-20 minutes a day in his/her workout to flexibility. When they do it is not important except that it follows an activity that warms up their muscles such as, in the morning after a jog, after practice or at home in and after a warm shower. The athlete must be very flexible in their hip rotations, hurdle splits, lower back and hamstrings to be great.

How flexible does the athlete need to be? He/she should be so flexible that he/she can almost do a split! Sitting on the couch watching TV, or sitting on the computer or playing video games won't get them to this level of flexibility. To get where they need to be they will have to be disciplined to stretch twice a day. If the athlete isn't able to discipline himself/herself to do this – then suggest a yoga class.

In 25 years of coaching, I have found a direct correlation between hamstring problems and poor lower back flexibility. If you are running into this, address it with stretching and weight room exercises such as "good mornings" and "dead-lifts."

I watch young hurdlers and see many young hurdlers make many common mistakes that can lead to bad habits causing them to never achieve their potential. Some of these errors can very easily be corrected:

Hitting the Hurdle with the Lead Leg
Cause: Most often the hurdler's toe is pointed down (Plantar-Flexion) when attempting to clear the hurdle.
Fix: Keeping the toe pointed up (Dorsi-Flexion) at all times, will produce 2-3 inches in additional hurdle clearance.

Hitting the Hurdle with the Trail Leg

Cause: Most often the toe of the hurdler's "trail leg" is pointed down (Plantar-Flexion) when attempting to clear the hurdle. This downward pointing of the trail leg which is "plantar-flexion," decreases the ability of the hurdler to clear the hurdle by 2-3 inches.

Fix: Use "dorsi-flexion" and keep the toe up at all times.

Importance of Dorsi-flexion

A very important component to successful hurdling is "Dorsi-Flexion" (Heel up-Toe up) "Dorsi-Flexion" will allow the athlete to gain 2-3 inches in additional "lead leg" clearance and 2-3 inches in the "trail leg" clearance. It does not matter how tall an athlete is, if he or she is not using "Dorsi-Flexion" they will make themselves appear to be 4-6 inches shorter when they attack the hurdle. The end result is hitting the hurdle with either their lead and trail leg or both when attempting to go over the barrier.

Hitting the First Hurdle in the 110 Meter High's

The key to becoming a great 110 meter high hurdler is having a great transition from the starting blocks into the first hurdle. As you are aware, it is only 8 steps to the first hurdle. I see too many hurdlers hitting the first hurdle because they are not in good body position as they attack the hurdle. Unlike the sprint events the hurdler must be in a "Hips Tall" position by the either the 4th or 5th stride.

Failure to do so results in the athlete being 3-6 inches shorter than their normal body height and for that reason hits first hurdle. To be successful a hurdler must get into proper body alignment quickly. I would rather have the hurdler who is a tenth of a second slower going into the hurdle #1 but is in good body position, than to be faster and "over-rotated" at the hips.

Most hurdlers who are "over-rotated" at the hips and not in the "Hips-Tall" position cannot change their body posture once the race continues past the first hurdle.

Twisting or Slicing with the Lead Leg Action
Another bad habit that can cause hurdler problems is crossing the mid-point of the body with a lead arm. This causes the body to "compensate". At no time should the arms or legs cross the mid-point of the body. For example when the athlete takes his/her lead arm across past the mid-point of his body it causes the lead leg to hook or slice from below the waist.

The action that occurs below the waist is counter-balancing what happened above the waist resulting in wasted motion. Wasted motion hurts the athlete's speed performance.

Loss of Balance When Using the Trail Leg
Attempting to bring a trail leg over and through the hurdle can cause the athlete to lose balance for the same reason as above. When the athlete uses his lead arm and crosses the mid-point of his body either in front or behind, the athlete has to compensate for this negative movement by bringing the trail leg over the mid-point of his body. Again this is wasted motion. Inefficient movement causes the athlete to lose valuable time on each hurdle.

Dropping the Head When Attacking the Hurdle
I see many hurdlers dropping their head down as they attempt to clear the hurdle. Dropping the head from a normal "Neutral" head position can result in the hurdler banging or hitting the hurdle.

The elite hurdler's head position moves no more than 1-2 inches regardless of whether he/she is on top of the hurdle or running between them. Constant up and down head movement simply kills speed performance. When a hurdler drops his/her head suddenly, their center of mass drops 4-6 inches.

This results in more hurdles being hit by the athlete's lead and trail leg. Dropping the head can cause a hurdler that is 6' feet tall to perform like he/she is 5'-6" to 5'-8" inches tall. *The simple rule is stay "tall like a pencil" at all times. A pencil never changes its shape and always remains straight.*

Hitting Hurdles as the "Lead Leg" Leaves the Ground

Because the high hurdles in high school are only 39 inches tall, I find that most high school hurdlers are using a locked or straight lead leg. In college hurdles are 42 inches. Athletes that have not been taught proper "lead leg" technique will hit the higher hurdles until the lead leg action is re-learned. For the athlete to clear the hurdle with ease they must learn to leave the ground with the knee. This short lever helps the athlete to raise his/her "center of mass" 4-5 inches which aids in lead leg clearance of the hurdle. Also leading with the knee as the athlete leaves the ground also makes the lead leg action of the hurdler quicker. In summary, short levers are stronger and faster, while long levers are slower and less powerful.

Long & Slow Lead Arm Action (Arms away from the Body) Long and slow lead arm action is a problem many hurdlers have when they are on top of the hurdle. The hurdler's arms are wildly sweeping around the outside of the body and often pass into another hurdler's lane as the arm goes around behind their back. Often the athlete resembles an "airplane" with both arms extended away from the body.

Long levers are slow levers and cause the athlete to not get the arms into proper sprinting motion as they approach the ground. To correct such a flaw in technique, the hurdler needs to learn to keep simply keep his thumb pointed up as he/she attacks the hurdle. The "thumbs-up" motion will allow the hurdler to have a shorter and quicker lead arm action resulting in the hand stopping at the hip. Once the hand stops at the hip and the athlete hits the ground with both feet, he can continue "sprinting" with quick arm strokes between the hurdles.

Hitting the Last Hurdle Prior to the Finish

A very common problem is dropping the head and eyes as they go over the last hurdle to approach the finish line. Again, even at the end of the race it is important that the head always remain in a "neutral" head position. Athletes must first clear the hurdle then start the final sprint to the finish line.

The Race isn't Over Until It's OVER!

Remember just because the last hurdle has been cleared, the race isn't over! The most important 1.3 - 1.6 seconds are remaining so sprint through the finish!

Getting Run Down at the Finish Line

For some reason many athletes focus on "leaning" at the finish line. Contrary to popular belief, leaning is a "braking force" which causes the athlete to slow down before they hit the finish line. Athletes many times start leaning 5 to 8 meters prior to the finish line. Leaning too soon too long causes athletes to lose anywhere from .10 to .30 seconds. In conclusion the athlete should always run through the finish line and only think about decelerating 5 meters past the finish line. The timing clock stops when the athlete's torso "breaks the plane" at the finish. When the head, neck or arms cross the finish line it does not stop the clock.

Chopping Steps While Running Intermediate Hurdles

The top 25 hurdlers in the world know how to use both legs while hurdling. To be successful college and high school athletes must be willing to learn and use both legs while running the long hurdles. Chopping steps prior to clearing a hurdle kills both momentum and speed. If the hurdler is close to the hurdle and feels that his or her steps are going to be off, the correct thing to do is to accelerate 4-5 steps at an even higher rate of speed before they attempt to attach the hurdle. This sudden change in speed makes the athlete's hurdle steps come back into the proper pattern desired. Again chopping steps always kills a great hurdle time!

Methods of Changing Hurdle Technique

In conclusion the athlete must reformat his/her technique with many daily drills and lots of reps. The athlete cannot change the bad habits I have described with slow warm-up drills prior to practice. I recommend that the athlete use a mirror at home or in the weight room and practice 40-60 reps each day with the proper technique. The more reps that are done correctly enable the athlete to perfect his/her hurdle form for race day.

Remember bad habits that have been around for years cannot be changed overnight. Rome was not built in a day! If the athlete is patient and willing to work hard, anything can be changed.

If you would like to more information on hurdling please refer to my website:

SSEproducts.com

for my world class Elite Hurdle book & DVD "package" or my proven speed development program Book and DVD "package".

HURDLE TERMINOLOGY 101

By
Coach Steve Silvey
Assistant Track & Field Coach
Texas Tech University

Hips Tall position - Where the head, neck, back, and hips are in alignment. When leaving the starting blocks, the hurdler must be in a "Hips Tall" position no later than the 4th or 5th stride to insure proper hurdle clearance on the first barrier.

Dorsi-Flexion - Heel up/toe up at all times when running. Thru the use of "Dorsi-Flexion" the hurdler will gain 2-3 inches in *lead leg* clearance and *trail leg* clearance.

Flexibility - Flexibility is *key* to being a successful hurdler. The hurdler must be extremely flexible in the hip and groin area due to the physical demands of the event. The reality is the hurdler should be one of the most flexible athletes on the track team.

Tunnel Vision - Tunnel vision must be used by the hurdler for the entire race in order to not let distractions or other athletes interfere with his concentration and performance.

Neutral Head position - A "neutral" head position is the position your head is in when you are walking. A neutral head position must be used at all times.

Stretching - Stretching is vital to hurdling success - Elite Hurdlers stretch twice a day.

Maintain a level head position - The height of the hurdler's head position should never deviate whether they are on or off of the hurdle. There is no up and down motion. The head maintains a straight level line throughout the race.

Lead Arm Thumb Up - Arm movement is front to back with no side movement. By having the hurdler keeping his *lead* arm *thumb up* at all times much of the unnecessary arm motion or "air-planing" will be decreased.

Core Strength - The hurdler must have a great abdominal muscles or "Core Strength". A good core will help the athlete to fight off fatigue late in the race and to maintain proper technique.

Alternate Leg - The *alternate leg skill* is the ability to use either the left or right leg to clear the upcoming hurdle. All elite intermediate hurdlers must learn how to use both the right and left lead leg automatically as needed without thinking about it.

Elite *"CUTTING-EDGE"* Hurdling

by
Steve Silvey
Assistant Track & Field Coach
Sprints/Hurdles/Relays
Texas Tech University

There have been numerous articles written on the subject of proper hurdle technique. Many of these articles have never shared the nuts and bolts of actual hurdle workouts and what elite coaches can do to fine tune their athletes as they prepare for record setting performances.

Remember that a great male or female hurdler must spend a lot of time on **flexibility**. *The hurdler should be one of the most flexible athletes on the entire track and field team.* Be prepared to stretch twice a day. A tool that can be especially helpful is the Stretch-Rite Belt. It enables the athlete to get the same stretching benefits alone as they do when a coach or second athlete helps them to stretch.

Another important component to hurdling is **Dorsi-Flexion** (heel up-toe toe). Dorsi-Flexion will allow the athlete to gain 2-3 inches in additional "lead leg" clearance and 2-3 inches in "trail leg" clearance. Let's explore several key factors of hurdle training – specifically 110 meter high hurdle training.

1. Crowding the hurdles together
2. Lowering the hurdle height
3. Removing hurdles in training
4. Increasing attack velocity

Crowding the Hurdles Together
"Crowding the hurdles" together means moving the hurdles closer together than the original regulation marks on the track. For the men's 100-meter hurdle it means moving them to a distance of 8.5 meters instead of the normal regulation mark of 9.14 meters. For the women's 100-meter hurdle it means moving them to a distance of 8.0 – 7.5 meters instead of the normal regulation mark of 8.5 meters.

The purpose of crowding the hurdles together is to help the male and female athlete to develop the habit of getting the "lead leg" up faster to "attack" the hurdle. Once the hurdles have been adjusted and are "crowded", the result you should see is an athlete who is getting back into a "hips tall" position sooner as well as bringing the lead leg up to attack the hurdle quicker.

| Workout example for men: | 5 x 5 hurdles (8.5 meters) |
| Workout example for women: | 5 x 5 hurdlers (8.0 meters) |

While you are aware that a strong wind behind the sprinter running 100 and 200 meters will produce faster times, did you know that these same strong winds can cause the hurdler to crash and burn on the hurdles? Several years ago, prior to the Texas Relays, while I was coaching at the University of Arkansas, I spent 2-3 weeks crowding the hurdles in practice prepare my athletes for the strong "south breezes" that we always experience in Austin in March and April. As you probably know those "breezes" always "push" the athletes.

Harry Jones, a freshman hurdler from the University of Arkansas, worked very hard doing a lot of 8.5 meter hurdle training in practice. On the day of the competition, in the University division of the Texas Relays, Harry finished 2nd in a field of very talented athletes and the primary reason Harry accomplished this achievement in his freshman year was simply because he was able to put himself into better body position faster than other athletes. The strong winds caused many of the great college athletes who were also competing to crash and burn because of their inability to be in proper body position quickly. Harry later became the SEC Champion as a sophomore when he ran 13.69 FAT.

Lowering the Hurdle Height for 100/110 Event Practice
To help the athlete eliminate any fear of attacking hurdles during a race and achieve the proper "hips tall" position (like you see with elite athletes), drop the traditional 42" hurdle to 39" or even 36" in practice. By dropping the hurdle height in practice, the hurdler can get back to this proper "hips tall" position and will overcome the bad habits they may develop from the fear of a taller hurdle. Many young athletes have a tendency to "jump" the hurdle instead of "sprinting" through the hurdle.

When an athlete is "over rotated" at the hip, they are giving up a large share of their maximum leg power which in turn hurts the development of maximum speed performance for the hurdler. When I train my college male hurdlers, I drop the traditional 42" hurdle to 39" or even 36" in practice. Again, I do this to help the athlete learn how to quickly go into the "hips tall" position just like the elite sprinter.

Workout example:	College	8 x 10 Hurdles	39 inches
	High School Boys	6 x 10 Hurdles	36 inches
	High School Girls	5 x 10 Hurdles	30 inches

As a result of lowering the hurdles, you may be afraid the hurdler's lead leg height might get too low, but when you watch the hurdler often you will see that while racing the lead leg is often 2-3 inches too high above the hurdle. Not only will you see the hurdler attack the hurdles more efficiently but also can confidence as they overcome their fear of attacking the hurdles during a race.

There are other benefits to lowering hurdles as well. As you are aware a good hurdler will take 8 strides to the first hurdle and all hurdlers take 3 strides between hurdles. The *only* difference between the 13.5 hurdles and the 5.0 hurdle is the stride frequency of the athletes. Both athletes are taking the same number of strides while racing but the 13.5 hurdler is traveling at a much higher rate of speed. For this reason, I will have my college hurdlers who run the 42" hurdles for a meet go as low as 36" hurdles in practice so they can work on the *pure speed* that is required to be a great hurdler.

In order to avoid confusion, it's important to emphasize to the hurdler that we are lowering the hurdles for *speed development* and that they should not adjust to get down so low they make contact with the lower hurdles during the lower hurdle training.

The objectives of this drill are:

1. To overcome the fear of attacking the hurdle.
2. To be clean over the hurdle regardless of the hurdle height.
3. To develop maximum speed by running through the hurdles.

In 1997, while at the University of Arkansas, there was a young hurdler, Kevin White. The Sunday before the SEC Championships, he did the following high quality workout.

Workout	Hurdle Height	White's Time
1 x 10 hurdles	(39 inches)	13.1 – Hand
10 minute Recovery		
1 x 10 hurdles	(39 inches)	13.0 – Hand
10 minute Recovery		
1 x 10 hurdles	(39 inches)	12.9 – Hand

The following Saturday, Kevin White established a new SEC Meet Record with a "wind legal" 13.41 with FAT timing at the SEC Championship at Auburn University.

When lowering the hurdles for women who typically hurdle 30 – 33 inch hurdles in practice, go down to 28-30 inches to get the same effect and achieve the objectives mentioned above. The same objectives are true for men and women but remember when explaining the reason for lowering hurdles to the athlete the emphasis is on "speed" development.

At the University of Oregon, Micah Harris set the school record in 2002 with a 13.67. Much of his practice time was spent running over 39" hurdles. When I arrived I saw immediately Micah needed to learn how to sprint better. This drill was responsible for forcing him to sprint harder and faster between the hurdles in practice.

Eric Mitchum was only 18 when he arrived at the University of Oregon with what I would call an average high school sprint speed. He committed to doing a lot of the 36 and 39 inch "speed/hurdle" drills and finished second in the PAC-10 Championships with a 13.73 clocking and was only beaten by the eventual NCAA Champion, Ryan Wilson of USC. Eric's clocking was the fastest that I had ever coached as a true freshman. Before Eric, my fastest freshman was Eddie Jackson (University of Arkansas) who just missed the NCAA Final in 2000 when he ran 13.75.

Removing Hurdles
Occasionally, I will remove a hurdle from the set of hurdles in practice. Doing so will help the athlete to *increase their speed velocity* to the next hurdle. Please note that the intent is **not** to change the number of steps a hurdler uses between the hurdles. Instead it is to help the hurdler to handle *positive changes in speed* as they get ready to hurdle the next barrier.

Sample workout: 5 x 10 hurdles (remove hurdle #2)

Removing hurdle #2 causes the athlete to carry more speed into hurdles 3, 4, and 5. This allows the hurdler to actually *feel* what could happen in racing when there is a positive adrenalin release or during the natural speeding up of the race by the leaders when they attempt to win a race.

Attack Velocity
You can also help a hurdler's "attack velocity" by putting another starting line back behind the traditional starting mark of 13.72 meters. From the new mark the hurdler is now taking 10 steps to the first hurdle instead of 8.

At 10 steps, the hurdler is now carrying more speed into the first hurdle thus enabling him/her to have more speed going into hurdles 3, 4 and 5.

Workout example: 200 meters (70%)
                     5 x 5 hurdles (39 inches)
                     "Using Attack Velocity 10 steps"

As mentioned above, the regular distance from the starting line to the first hurdle for a male athlete is 13.72 meters. However, when using this "attack velocity" concept the new starting line is 16.50 meters from the first hurdle. Women hurdlers will use the same distance as the men from the start to the first hurdle to increase their "attack velocity."

Coaching the 300 Intermediate Hurdler

Did you know that the top 25 300 meter hurdlers in the world *can use both their right and left legs* when running the 300 meter hurdles? The ability to use either leg as needed in hurdling is not a skill they use regularly but instead have developed it to use as needed in emergency situations such as, fatigue, headwinds, or hitting a previous hurdle. They are so adept with this skill that immediately and instinctively without even a conscious effort they can use the opposite leg and make their race a success. For this reason, I strongly believe in the benefit of learning to use alternate legs and which is why my 300 and hurdlers work on this skill. All of my male hurdlers start learning this skill beginning in the fall. We continue working on it during the winter and early spring by doing many "4" stepping over the women's 100 meter hurdles. This simply means that the athlete is going to "right lead" on one hurdle and then "left lead" on the next hurdle. This will feel uncomfortable and awkward at first but if an athlete is doing 10 x 10 hurdles 3-4 days a week at a low rate of speed in their training shoes during a warm-up or cool-down, they will learn this new skill and become comfortable with using alternate legs for hurdling.

Calvin Davis, a 400 meter runner had never touched a hurdle in his life before 1996 and wasn't sure he wanted to. We made the decision it was in his best interest to convert to hurdling. He ran many of these 10 x 10 hurdles in practice (with the R-L) 4-step drill. Calvin ran his first race as a hurdler in April of 1996 with a time of 49.29. Later in August in just the 15th race of his life, he won the Olympic Bronze with a personal best of 47.91. Not a bad accomplishment for the man who just a short year before had said "no" to trying the hurdles.

Lowering the Intermediate Hurdle Height – 300 Hurdles

Dropping the intermediate hurdles 3-6 inches will allow the hurdler to be aggressive in practice because he/she will gain confidence that will carry the hurdler through the meet. If you are trying to convert a 400 or 800 meter runner to the 300/400 meter hurdles, you can help them to overcome any fear and "feel" success by dropping the hurdle in practice. I personally like to do this on the hurdles on one or both curves in the 400 meters and on the hurdle on the only curve the 300 hurdler runs. Many times I don't even tell the young hurdler that I have dropped the hurdle height 3-6 inches. Why? Because it is very important for an athlete to *feel success* in practice....when an athlete feels success that feeling will carry over in to track meets.

Removing Intermediate Hurdles

I often remove a few hurdles in training sessions for two main reasons:

1. Force athletes to use alternate lead legs
2. Improve training performance times to remove psychological barriers

In a workout, I recommend removing the first 2 or 3 hurdles to force the athletes to, first, run the distance and second, use whichever legal leg comes up as the approach that particular hurdle. This forces the hurdler to practice using the opposite leg and become comfortable with doing so. In addition, I emphasize that they must run the distance. Chopping their steps is not an option and should be something they are instructed to *not* consider doing.   The rule is simple: Whatever leg comes up is the leg to use!

Workout Sample:	150 Meters (70%)
1 x 8 hurdlers	(Remove hurdles #1 & #2)

I have also been known to remove the final one, two or three hurdles for the intermediate hurdler. When I do this, my instructions to the hurdler are very simple: your goal is to finish the hurdle interval faster than ever before and you can because you have no hurdles in your way to the finish line! My experience is that this is a great for confidence building exercise particularly for the young hurdler. It gets them into the mindset of covering their race distance in a lifetime best in practice and then they carry that great confident mindset straight into the track meet.

A confident mindset plus the extra adrenalin that naturally occurs prior to a meet means that the athlete's time is now ready to drop a second or two when they are in that big race and ready to compete hard. If an athlete can run fast in practice, I believe it will be easy for them to run fast in those important late season track meets.

During the 2002 season at the University of Oregon, I had the opportunity to coach a young athlete named Brandon Holiday who was a walk-on at Oregon. Brandon was an average practice runner with a personal best of 52.97. In practice Brandon's times improved steadily from 52 to 51 to 50.0. Late in May, Brandon ran a big personal best and became the PAC-10 400 hurdle champion with an electronic time of 50.73. His speed that had remained unchanged increased steadily when I started in mid-season removing one or two hurdles over the final 100 meters of his race and/or lowering the height of the last hurdles. By removing or changing the height of the hurdles, Brandon was able to see and feel success even when he was in his greatest stages of fatigue.

Workout Sample #1:

> 200 Meters (70%)
> 1 x 8 hurdles (remove hurdle #6 & #7)
> 3 x 3 hurdles (at relaxed goal pace)

Workout Sample #2:

> 1 x 8 hurdles (remove last 2 hurdles & sprint home)= Goal Pace
> 2 x 5 hurdles (at relaxed goal pace)

Workout Sample #3:

> 1 x 9 hurdles "sprint home" remove final hurdle=goal pace
> 15 minute break
> 2 x 3 hurdles (at relaxed goal pace)

Hopefully you have found some of this information helpful and will be able to incorporate it into your hurdle program. In addition, these items will help you as a coach:

- **World Class Hurdle Training program (Book and DVD)**
- World Class "All Sports" Speed Training Program (Book & DVD)
- Coach Silvey's "Texas Tech" Training Program (Cook Book) Workouts for entire year
- Coach Silvey's "Arkansas" Training program (Cook Book)

Check out my website at: **SSEproducts.com**

Learning How to Alternate Lead Legs For The 300/400 Hurdles

by
Coach Steve Silvey
Sprints/Hurdles/Relays
Texas Tech University

The top 25 hurdlers in the world know how to alternate their lead legs when needed. Top athletes may not *want* to switch legs during a race but are able to do son in an emergency situation. They have done the work necessary to be prepared to meet this challenge when the wrong leg inevitably comes up prior to a hurdle.

Every athlete favors using a certain leg when hurdling but having the ability and confidence to use the opposite leg enables the athlete to run a great race when any one of the following occurs:

1. They start out too fast
2. They are running into strong headwind
3. They hit the previous hurdle

As a coach who had the opportunity to coach the 1991 World Champion for the 400 meter hurdles and both the Olympic Silver and Bronze Medalists in the 400 meter hurdles at the 1996 Olympic Games, I am a firm believer that the 300/400 meter hurdler will never become a great intermediate hurdler unless he/she can master using both legs.

The following is a very simple drill to help athletes become great in the 300/400 hurdles:

Men: Set hurdles up on the women's 100 meter hurdles marks (8.5 Meters   apart).   The athlete may wear either their spikes or training flats. The athlete will now use four strides between each hurdle. This means they will use their right leg on one hurdle and their left leg on their next hurdle.

The goal is to do: **10 times x 10 hurdles (3 times a week)**

The height of the hurdle should start at 30 inches and may go higher and higher as the hurdler masters the drill. Do this drill either at the beginning of the workout or at end of the workout. Do this drill 2-3 times a week and watch the hurdler master both legs in only a few weeks.

Women: Do the same drill as above, but place the hurdles at either 7.0 or 7.5 meters apart. This will allow the women hurdlers to alternate right/left leg on every other hurdle. Be sure to set these hurdles at 30 inches in height, to start with and raise the hurdles as they improve.

I taught Calvin Davis (a non-hurdler) to do this drill and in a period of only 8 months, in only his 15th race of his life, he won the Olympic Bronze Medal at the 1996 Olympic Games.

If the 300/400 hurdler can learn to use both legs automatically without thinking, they never have to worry about having a bad race as they will be able to adjust to the obstacles that often can occur in this grueling race.

Best of luck!

PACE CHART
110 Meter High & 100 Meter Hurdles

Hurdle #1	2.2	2.2	2.3	2.4	2.5
Split	.9	1.0	1.1	1.2	1.3
Hurdle #2	3.1	3.2	3.4	3.6	3.8
Split	.9	1.0	1.1	1.2	1.3
Hurdle #3	4.0	4.2	4.5	4.8	5.1
Split	.9	1.0	1.1	1.2	1.3
Hurdle #4	5.0	5.2	5.6	6.0	6.4
Split	1.0	1.0	1.1	1.2	1.3
Hurdle #5	6.0	6.2	6.4	7.2	7.7
Split	1.0	1.0	1.1	1.2	1.3
Hurdle #6	7.0	7.2	7.8	8.4	9.0
Split	1.0	1.0	1.1	1.2	1.2
Hurdle #7	8.0	8.2	8.9	9.6	10.2
Split	1.0	1.0	1.1	1.2	1.2
Hurdle #8	9.1	9.2	10.0	10.8	11.4
Split	1.1	1.0	1.1	1.2	1.2
Hurdle #9	10.2	10.3	11.1	12.0	12.6
Split	1.1	1.1	1.1	1.2	1.2
Hurdle #10	11.3	11.4	12.2	13.2	13.8
Split	1.1	1.1	1.1	1.2	1.2
Run In	1.5	1.6	1.6	1.7	1.7
Total Time	12.80	13.00	13.80	14.90	15.50

300 Meter Hurdle Pace Chart

Hurdle	Distance	Time										
#1	45 Meters	5.7	5.9	6.0	6.1	6.3	6.4	6.5	6.7	6.9	7.1	7.3
#2	80 Meters	9.7	10.0	10.2	10.4	10.7	10.9	11.1	11.5	11.9	12.3	12.6
#3	115 Meters	13.7	14.1	14.4	14.7	15.1	15.4	15.7	16.3	16.9	17.5	17.9
#4	150 Meters	17.7	18.2	18.6	19.0	19.5	19.9	20.3	21.1	21.9	22.6	23.3
#5	185 Meters	21.7	22.3	22.8	23.3	23.9	24.4	25.0	25.9	26.9	27.8	28.7
#6	220 Meters	25.8	26.5	27.1	27.7	28.4	29.0	29.8	30.8	32.0	33.1	34.2
#7	255 Meters	29.9	30.8	31.5	32.1	32.9	33.7	34.7	35.9	37.2	38.4	39.8
#8	290 Meters	34.2	35.2	39.9	36.8	37.6	38.5	39.7	41.1	42.5	43.9	45.4
Finish	**300 Meters**	**35.5**	**36.6**	**37.3**	**38.2**	**39.0**	**40.0**	**41.2**	**42.8**	**44.3**	**45.8**	**47.4**

THE

STARTING

BLOCKS

Starting Blocks 101

By
Coach Steve Silvey
Championship SSE Products
Dallas, Texas

Power Foot - The power foot is found on the athlete's strongest leg. The athlete's 'power foot' should be placed in the *front* starting block.

Quick-Side Foot - The 'Quick-Side Foot' is located on the quickest side of the athlete's body. Place the 'Quick-Side Foot' foot in the *back* starting block.

Quick Side Testing – A simple test is used to find the quickest side of the athlete's body.

1) The athlete places both hands down on the sides of his/her body against his/her hips.
2) The coach says "Go"!
3) The athlete slaps his/her hands very quickly across his/her chest leaving his/her hands on his/her chest.
4) The coach looks at the hand placement and determines which hand has touched the athlete's body first.

The hand that touches the body first is considered the "Quick Side" of the athlete's body. The slower hand is then considered the "Power Side" of the athlete's body.

Placement of Front Starting Block – The placement of the *front* starting block should equal 1.5 to 2 of the athlete's shoe size in distance from the starting line.

Placement of Back Starting block - The placement of the *back* starting block should be 2.5 to 3 feet in distance from the starting line.

Stretch Reflex – Stretch reflex is the position of the calf muscle and Achilles tendon that maximizes momentum. The effect is similar to pulling the rubber band way back and releasing it – the rubber band flies across the room. When the rubber band isn't stretched is falls to the ground and goes nowhere because it has no momentum.

Angle of Starting Blocks – The angle of the starting blocks should be at a 45 degree angle to maximize the "stretch reflex" of the calf muscle and the Achilles tendon. Even though the smaller the angle the greater the stretch reflex, the athlete would not be able to get their foot on the pedal. The 45 degree angle enables the athlete to explode once the gun goes off.

Foot Placement on Starting Blocks - On the ground prior to the set position the athlete should have his/her foot touching the block pedals. The athlete should dig the front two spikes of his/her shoe into the track and place the rest of the foot on the block pedal to again maximize the *"stretch-reflex"* of the lower leg.

Hand Placement for Starting Blocks - The athlete should be on his/her fingertips with the hand located 2-3 inches in front of the shoulders and 2-3 inches outside of the knee so that when the athlete starts to take off and is swinging his/her arms, he/she will not hit his/her knee. If the athlete places his/her hands too far away from the body he/she will lose the ability to produce "maximum arm drive" as he/she leaves the starting blocks.

Angle of Legs in "Set Position" - In the "set position" the rear leg is lifted off of the ground. Both legs are flexed. The front leg is 90 degrees at the knee and the back leg 120 to 135 degrees.

Apply Pressure to the Starting Blocks - The athlete is in the "set position" and places foot pressure against *both* block pedals. The athlete's hips are raised slightly above the shoulders.

Eye Position In Starting Blocks - The sprinter's eyes should not be focused on any one point. Instead the athlete should be looking out 2-3 feet ahead on the track.

Head Position in Starting Blocks -The sprinter's head should always remain down in a relaxed "neutral" head position. *The head should remain relaxed at all times.*

Position of Shoulders in the "Set" Position -The athletes should place their blocks in a comfortable position that will allow them to have their shoulders actually 2-3 inches behind the hands. This will allow the athlete to have better block contact as well as produce great force application once the gun goes off.

Locking the Hips in the "Set Position" – Locking the hips in the "set position" is the ability for the athlete to totally lock out his hips when he/she is in the "set position." When the athlete is in the "set position" and at the last moment tightens or squeezes his abdominal muscles. This action forces the hips to move backwards an additional 2-3 inches. "Locking the hips" it the "set position" enables the athlete to have 100% force application against the block pedals once he or she hears the sound of the starting gun.

Correct Foot Placement When Driving From Blocks - The athlete does not have an ample amount of time to do the normal running cycle. The athlete's initial 4-5 steps out of the blocks will actually land slightly behind the knee instead of under the knee. Because of the shortness of the stride, this low heel recovery allows for a quick placement of the first step to the track. The front leg extends forcefully to provide a strong drive. Those first short steps aid the athlete in creating more power as he drives out of the starting blocks. The athlete's stride will continue to grow in length and frequency during the first four to five strides.

Stumbling as the Athletes Come out of the Starting Blocks –Stumbling is caused when the athlete is taking either too long of a stride as he/she leaves the block or because he/she is taking a stride that is outside of their "center of mass". Outside of the "center of mass is usually a step that is thrown outside the athlete's shoulder and lands near the edge of the athlete's lane. The end result is a slow step that creates no power and often the results in the athlete stumbling.

Using the Upper Body to Drive Effectively from the Starting Blocks - To ensure a strong drive out of the starting blocks, the athlete must position his/her hands to be on the fingertips placed 2-3 inches directly in front of the shoulders. When the athlete hears the gun, he/she strongly punches the arm/hand of the front starting foot forward. At the same time the athlete punches the hand of the back starting foot hand backwards. The "driving of the arms" initiates the start from the starting blocks

Action vs. Reaction - This is a basic law of physics, in which the more "force application" the athlete places against the block pedals the greater the force they have to propel themselves forward away from the starting blocks. If the athlete doesn't push strongly against the pedals there is no need to use starting blocks. A common mistake seen with young athletes is that they step off the pedals instead of driving hard against the pedals to get the momentum they need to propel them forward.

Stimulating the Fast Twitch Muscle Fibers Prior to the Start – Before entering the blocks, the athlete should do several "jump-tucks" in the air to stimulate the fast twitch muscle fibers in the lower legs. Those are the muscles used during the starting process. Doing the "jump-tucks" prepares the athlete's body to be on auto-pilot when the gun goes off.

Relaxation in the Starting Blocks – It is important for the athlete to be totally relaxed prior to the start of the race. To do this, the athlete should position himself/herself in the starting blocks then take 2-3 deep breaths. Last but not least he/she should be prepared to be held 3-4 seconds once in the "set position" prior to the gun sounding. Athletes that cannot hold themselves in the "set position" for that length of time are not properly relaxed.

Jumping the Gun – Prior to the race it is important that the athlete work on his/her concentration. Once the athlete in is in the "set position" and before the gun sounds, the athlete must be patient and concentrate on listening for the gun so he/she can react instantly when he/she hears the sound of the gun. If the athlete isn't mentally prepared he/she will not be focused and usually "jump the gun". Jumping the gun = disqualified. "Jumping the gun" is a sign the athlete is not mentally prepared for the race and is concentrating too hard on the wrong thing or not concentrating at all.

SPRINT TRAINING FOR THE 100 Meters & 200 Meters

SPEED
DEVELOPMENT TRAINING SYSTEMS

The three types of SPEED Energy Systems I use in Speed training are:

a. **Speed** (Under 50 yards or meters)

b. **Speed ONE** (Over 50 yards or meters but under 100 yards or meters)

c. **Speed Endurance** (Over 100 yards or meters)

To improve SPEED you must address all three of these Speed Energy Systems in training

Effort is 90-95% and recovery is critical. Use a standing, three-point or crouched start. Speed training needs to be done prior to weight training or regular football practice. ***THE KEY TO RUNNING FAST IS STAYING RELAXED!***

Example of a Speed Training Workout:

2 x (40 meters, 40 meters, 40 meters)

- ➢ **Effort: 90-95%**
- ➢ **Run one athlete at a time**
- ➢ **Record a Time for each athlete**
- ➢ **Rest interval: 2-3 Minutes**
- ➢ **Rest Interval Between sets 8-10 Minutes**

SPEED involves the numerous areas of the body - muscle groups, circulation (blood supply to these muscles), the mind and most importantly the central nervous system. As an athlete prepares the body for *speed*, he/she must develop his/her motor skills so the necessary components for *speed* are stored as muscle memory.

The Speed Drills and Techniques that I teach my athletes must be learned and perfected at a slow rate of speed first gradually increasing until the athlete can perform them correctly but at faster rate of speed. After the athlete has mastered the drills and techniques, they can increase their range of motion and stride rate. For an athlete to become fast and stay fast, we must utilize their fast twitch muscles regularly. We must continue to stimulate the body's fast twitch muscle fibers.

SPEED

IF YOU DON'T USE IT,

THEN YOU LOSE IT!

SPEED GOAL

**Continue to Develop,
Use
&
Stimulate
the Body's
Fast-Twitch
Muscle Fibers
on a Regular Basis
to improve
SPEED!**

CAN YOU REALLY BECOME FASTER?

by
Coach Steve Silvey
University of Arkansas

Many of us as athletes and Coaches believe athletes are born with a certain amount of *SPEED* and nothing can really help to change this God-given quality. I personally do not agree with this myth, As a Coach of the 2000's, I believe and have seen that all athletes can become faster if we take the time to learn more about some of the basics concepts of *SPEED* training which are available. I am on a mission to learn as much as I can about this topic.

All Athletes do have a certain number of fast-twitch muscle fibers available to allow our bodies to become faster, but I feel that we often do nothing to actively stimulate these fast-twitch muscle fibers into performing at top end SPEED on a regular basis. As I have mentioned before one of my previous articles with regards to fast twitch muscle fibers:

IF YOU DON'T USE IT, YOU LOSE IT!

This means that we must do fast but relaxed *SPEED* training at 90-95% once the athletes are in good physical condition, to help in programming these fast-twitch muscle fibers to "fire" quickly when needed on a regular basis.

While the head track and field coach at Blinn College (1987-1994). I coached a young man named Timmy Montgomery, a 10.61 high school sprinter from Gaffney, South Carolina. Montgomery became exposed to SPEED Training, drills and strength training that enabled him to run 9.96 (FAT) and win the JUCO National Championship in the 100 meters. I have also conducted numerous **SPEED** training camps and over a 3-4 day period, have had numerous athletes improve their 40 yards times by .2 to .3 seconds.

I honestly believe a vast majority of *"shin splints"* are caused by improper foot mechanics.

I have been blessed to have learned a lot about how athletes are prepared at a very young age to adapt their body to sports by the use of numerous sports drills. I have noticed a lot of the U.S. Athletes, if at all, 4-6 years later than their foreign counterparts. I firmly believe these athletes, having been introduced to these type of Speed, coordination and rhythm, resistance drills and plyometrics before the age of 15, are much more adapted to excelling at sports where SPEED is a factor.

My question to all of you coaches and athletes: Isn't *SPEED* a very important quality to the success of your sports? Then what are you doing on a regular basis to prepare the Athletes to become faster? What will more SPEED do for a football, basketball or baseball player who has the desire to go to college on an athletic scholarship or make it to the Pro's?

I firmly believe that with regards to an athletes SPEED everything starts from the ground and works up. For the athletes to excel in SPEED DEVELOPMENT, he must first learn to use "Dorsi-flexion" with the foot. This term is merely keeping the toe up through the use, stretching the calf muscle. Then that foot in the dorsi flexion position is pulled through to the buttocks and then placed on the ground under the knee. You must understand that for the athlete to become quicker, "Dorsi-Flexion" is needed to quicken this amount of time the athlete spends on the ground.

If the athlete refuses to do this and keeps their toes pointed down, then the term is called "Planter-flexion" is used which is very bad! This is because this forces the athlete to use a breaking effect then the come in contact with the ground.

This breaking effect caused him to become slower because it almost like putting the brakes on in a car. Pointing the toe down when attempting to run fast, puts an unnecessary strain on the hamstring and the shins! I honestly believe a vast majority of "shin splints" are caused by improper foot mechanics. Athletes should run on the balls of their feet (Widest part of Shoe) at all times. Nothing good ever happens by running on you heels, unless you are planning on running a marathon!

Once the athlete's foot leaves the ground, it is cycled backwards or pulled up at the buttocks. At this point the foot is then brought back down to the ground underneath the knee. So many coaches tell their athletes to lengthen their stride which again causes a breaking effect by "Over-striding" which then causes a loss of power. For the athlete to utilize 100% of his body power capacities, he must run tall and keep all parts of his body near or under his "Center of Mass" at all times.

I see many athletes that might be 6 feet tall in height and run 3-5 inches shorter, because they are "over-rotating" at the hips. This causes a 20-30% loss in true SPEED performance.

With regards to arm action, the athlete must move them in a quick and efficient manner where the hand stops at the chin or shoulder and then moves down and stops at the side of the hip. It is important that you realize a short long lever is a slower lever. To run fast, the athlete must have a "piston" type arm motion to maximize their *SPEED!*

One key point is for the arms to never cross the mid-point of the body. This "Mid-point" in when you draw a line down the body to separate it into two equal parts. Crossing the mid-point with either the arms or legs will cause slowing down of SPEED performance because of the lack of efficiency.

With regards to the shoulders, they must be kept low and relaxed at all times. The same holds true for the face which must be relaxed with a loose and relaxed jaw muscle. The Head should remain in a "Neutral" position and all times. This means the eyes should be looking forward down the field or track 30-40 yards.

As a coach who is against the use of illegal performance enhancing drugs, such as steroids or human growth hormones, because of their long term negative effects, I have tried to learn a lot more about "Super-Nutrition".

I have been able to work closely with a pharmaceutical company to produce several products that can help athletes with poor nutrition habits. One such product is **Phosphate Plus** which aids the body in minimizing lactic acid build-up, cramps and even muscle pulls or strains. Also **Osteo-Tech** a product that helps with natural muscle contraction and aids in preventing stress fractures.

I have recently completed my "NEW" second addition of the World Class "All Sports" Speed Development Program (Book & DVD) which consists of entirely new 16 week *SPEED* Training Program for football players and also a 16 week training program for the 100/200 meter sprinter. These items can be purchased thru my company Championship SSE Products. The website is: ***SSEproducts.com*** or by calling (972) 294-5696.

Sprint Training for the 100/200 Meters

By
Coach Steve Silvey
The University of Oregon

Many coaches believe that athletes are born "God-Given' SPEED and nothing can be done to change it. As a coach with over twenty years experience at the high school, junior college and university levels, I strongly disagree with
This statement, To the contrary, I have found anything is possible with an athlete who has above average talent and who is willing to,

- Train Hard
- Focus on the right things-doing all of the little things before the workout-such as, correct warm-up and cool down procedure, proper nutrition and hydration, applying good sleep habits and additional flexibility work.

One example of this theory is the former National Junior College Record Holder and Champion Tim Montgomery (9.96). In the spring of 1993, I met and persuaded Tim to sign a scholarship to run for my junior college program at Blinn College in Brenham, Texas. At the time Tim was a very thin high school sprinter from Gaffney, South Carolina. As a high school senior with a mere (electronic timed) 100 meter best of 10.61 FAT, Montgomery was not even ranked as one of the nations 'Top 25 High School Sprinters'. Montgomery's high school track team was so small that they could not field a 400 meter relay, so Tim did not have the opportunity to learn 400 Relay exchanges.

When Montgomery arrived at Blinn College in the fall of 1993 he was 5-10" and weighed a mere 128 pounds. He definitely did not fit the definition of a typical high school sprinter or typically what we looked for when we recruit. What Montgomery did have was great family support mechanism and a super positive attitude. Montgomery came to Brenham, Texas with hunger to be the best he could be. Along with his positive Attitude, he brought with him great daily work habits.

Tim had the right attitude; he trained hard and focused on the right things. First he focused ands trained to improve his overall body strength, basic flexibility and running technique thru many hours of drills. Early in the spring of 1994 at the Sun angel Classic at Arizona State University, Montgomery ran a 20.1 lead off leg on our 4 x 200 meter Relay that ran 1:21.45. That time beat a number of collegiate powers as LSU, USC and UCLA and several world class track clubs. Later that spring in Odessa Texas he beat Nigerian World Class Sprinter Daniel Effiong of Central Arizona CC in a meet record 9.96 seconds. It was thought to be a "NEW"

World Junior Record beating the record of 10.07 by one of my former recruits to Texas A&M University recruits, Andre Cason who I recruited in 1987, but the track had to be measured with a steel tape and came up 2 inches short according to the IAAF guidelines.

PROPER RUNNING MECHANICS-Through the use of proper solid running mechanics, the athlete will become more efficient with regards to his movement of body parts. An athlete who is quick and efficient will be able to improve his own athletic performance. Types of running mechanic drills are as follows:

1. Speed Drills

2. Hurdle-Rhythm Drills

Leg power is necessary for speed. For an athlete to be able to maximize 100% of his leg power capabilities, the athlete must run "HIPS TALL" over his hips at all times and keep all parts of his body near or under the "center of mass" at all times. I often see many young athletes shrink 3-6 inches while running because they are over-rotating at the hips. This causes a loss of 20%-30% of leg power and a substantial loss in true SPEED performance.

The athlete must also have a tremendous amount of lower leg strength (below the waist) because each time the athlete strikes the ground he is applying three (3) times his body weight to the ground. The coaching cues when working on proper running mechanics that I use with my athletes on a regular daily basis are:

- **Toe-Up**
- **Heel-Up**
- **Knee-Up**
- **Chest-Up**
- **Head-Up**
- **Eyes-Up**

Most importantly the athletes must remain in "Hips-Tall" position at all times for the 6 coaching cues listed above to be effective. The athlete that does not stay in proper body position over his hips will give up 20-30% of their maximum leg power. This is a common fault of young athletes that have not been instructed properly.

Barefoot running is an essential part of a "complete" conditioning program. It is useful in order to strengthen the athlete's tendons, ligaments and small muscle groups of the feet. Training shoes act as a mere cast and do nothing to strengthen the foot.

When it comes to an athlete's *SPEED*, it starts from the ground up. First, for any athlete to excel in Speed Development, he or she must learn to use *"Dorsi Flexion"* with his/her foot. Unfortunately, most young athletes use *"Plantar Flexion"* instead. *"Plantar Flexion"* is a BAD habit. Because this downward pointing of the toe causes a breaking effect upon contact with the ground it is similar to continually "riding" the brakes in a moving car. *"Plantar Flexion"* keeps the athlete's foot on the ground too long, maximizing ground time which translates into slower speed performance. In addition the "braking effect" can put a lot of strain on the ankle, shin, and most of all the hamstring muscles. In my opinion, *"Plantar Flexion"* is the number one cause of "Shin Splints" and Hamstring Injuries.

Hamstring injuries are very common in sports that involve speed. In my opinion the hamstring muscle is the weakest muscle in the body. "Plantar Flexion" increases hamstring weakness. It is important to emphasize strengthening the hamstring muscles one leg at a time as well working on lower back flexibility by spending focused time to strengthen these areas. In addition to the problems caused by "Plantar Flexion" I feel that many hamstring injuries are caused by poor lower back flexibility and this is an area that is often neglected by the athlete.

Great Speed Performance starts with ***"Dorsi-Flexion"***. "Dorsi-Flexion" is keeping the toe and heel up while running. The runner is literally stretching the calf muscle while running. When running the athlete pulls the heel tight "through to the buttocks" and then places it on the ground under the knee. When the athlete's foot lands on the track surface or the ground, the foot is then cycled backwards or pulled up to the buttocks. At this point, the foot is then brought back down to the ground with again, the toe up, as it makes contact with the ground underneath the knee. A common mistake made by coaches is to tell their athletes to take "longer strides". "Over-striding" causes a "braking effect" as the athlete often lands on his heel and the athletes also lose *power*.

How does the use of "***Dorsi-Flexion***" make an athlete faster and why is it better than "Plantar Flexion"? Dorsi-Flexion makes an athlete much more active upon contact with the ground or track and also allows the athlete to "get-off" the ground or track surface quicker. *"Rome was not built in a day"* and don't expect your athletes to pick up this new technique overnight. The bad habits of athletes took years to develop and it will take him/her weeks to correct it, but once the athlete learns "Dorsi-Flexion", then he/she will be much more efficient in landing. Efficient landing minimizes both ground time and air time which translates into faster speed performances. Again but not using proper Dorsi-Flexion it creates the following negatives:

- More Strain on the hamstring muscles
- Braking effect at ground contact
- Increased ground contact time
- Hinders Speed performance

To run fast an athlete must run on the balls of his/her feet at all times. This means landing on the "widest part" of the front of their foot each and every time. Athletes must also learn how to strengthen the tendons, ligaments and small muscle groups in the foot, ankle and below the knee if they are to be able to run on their toes. An athlete's body cannot be supported unless these areas are strong. Good exercises to strengthen the feet are:

1. Bare Foot Running
2. Sand-Pit Plyometrics
3. Weight Training exercises focusing below the knee

If an athlete attempts to land and push off their heel, he/she can never master SPEED. **Remember:** *Unless you plan on running a marathon nothing good ever happens on your heel.*

Proper arm action is important for *speed* as well. The athlete must move the arms in a quick and efficient manner stopping the hand near the chin on the upward motion and at the hips on the downward motion. **Remember!** *A short level is a quick lever; a long lever is a slow lever.* To run fast the athlete must have a "Piston" type arm motion to maximize their SPEED! Two key points you should take note are:

A. **The arms never cross the mid-point of the body.** Find the "mid-point" by drawing a line down the middle of your body to separate it into two equal parts. Crossing the mid-point with either the arms or the legs will cause slowing down of SPEED performance because of inefficiency of movement.

➢ Hands moving to the center line of the body at shoulder height and back to the hip.

B. **The elbows must be kept within 2- 4 inches of the body at all times.** If the arms are too far away from the body, this "Chicken

Wing" movement will cause the athlete to lose maximum SPEED performance.

➢ Arms should be at a loose 90 degree at the elbow
➢ Palms in and thumb up.
➢ Hands should never go any higher than shoulder height.
➢ Short levers are quicker and stronger levers.
➢ Always run with a stiff or locked wrist

It should be noted when the athlete flexes is hands when sprinting, it sends flexor messages as he runs down the football field or track. When he has his hands open but palms down and promotes the hand, it turns off the athletes' bicep muscles/ Using these flexors are bad and will hurt the athletes speed performance.

Last but certainly not least, is the posture for the upper body:

1. The shoulders should be kept low and relaxed at all times
2. The face and the jaw should remain relaxed.
3. The athlete's head should remain in its normal position which I refer to as "Neutral Head Position" as if he was merely standing in place.

If the athlete drops his head or eyes slightly when running, it hinders the ability for a nice high knee lift while running. By dropping the head, the athletes now lowers his center of mass causing a domino effect on the rest of his body which in turn causes his performance level to decline. To help the athlete keep his head up, have him raise his eyes and look forward 30-50 yards. Have him focus on an object that is 6-8 feet above the ground that is located past the finish line. Examples of this would be a tree, building or a set of windows. Doing this ensures that the athlete's head and hips remain tall throughout the entire distance run or the race.

For great track and field training books and "Legal Nutritional Supplements go to my website"
I suggest the following books that were written for high school coaches!

- **45 minute Workout-Running Events (Book & DVD)**
- **55 Minute Workout-Field Events (Book)**
- **60 Minute Workout-Cross Country (Book)**
- **World Class "All Sports" Speed Training Program**

Website: SSEproducts.com

TEN ESSENTIALS FOR SPEED IMPROVEMENT

By
Coach Steve Silvey
University of Oregon

Run with Heel-up and Toe-up at all times (DORSI-FLEXION) & stay relaxed at all times!

The athlete should land and push off the front part of the foot at all times. (Nothing Good Happens on Your Heels)

Relax your FACE & JAW at all times.

Head Should Be in a "NUETRAL" head position at all times.

Shoulders should remain at normal position while running.

Elbows should remain close to the body at all times.

Hands should never cross the mid-point of the body at any time!

Arm Motion should be short and fast "LIKE A PISTON". Hands should stop move up & down fast from the chin shoulder to the hip.

While running, the athlete's foot should land slightly in front of the hips. The athlete should never over-stride, as this will decrease the athletes leg power. (FREQUENCY IS THE KEY TO SPEED)

The athlete should always remain in a "Hips Tall" position. If the Athlete leans too far forward, they will shrink in height when running. This "over rotating" of the hips will cause the athlete to lose 20-30% of their hip & leg power.

ATTACKING THE 200 METERS
by
Coach Steve Silvey
Sprints/Hurdles/Relays
Texas Tech University

Top 8 200 Meter Runners Coach by Steve Silvey

Jason Hendrix	Blinn College	20.25
Derrick Thompson	Arkansas	20.31
Henry Neal	Blinn College	20.40
Aham Okeke	Blinn College	20.47
Melvin Lister	Arkansas	20.51
Tyree Gailes	Texas Tech	20.57
Trevor Rush	Arkansas	20.58
Ricardo Greenidge	Blinn College	20.63

The 200 meters while considered a long sprinting event is unique due to the fact that in order to excel in the event and be great the athlete must have the,

➢ Speed of a 100 meter runner
➢ Strength of a 400 meter runner
➢ "Aggressiveness" of an NFL middle linebacker

In addition the athlete must run "smart." The 200 meters is split into equal parts. The first 100 meters is run on the curve. The second half is on a straightaway. To run this race takes an effective strategy.

At the Division 1 level I believe it is vital for the athlete to attack from the start by "getting the jump" on the rest of the field during the first 60-70 meters of the race when they are running on the curve. Being aggressive from the start around the curve often translates into an "edge" going into the straightaway where it is important to have the lead or "edge" on the rest of the field.

In 1993 one of my junior college athletes who no one knew or had ever heard of, Jason Hendrix of Tatum Texas, used this strategy at the USA National Championships. Hendrix blasted off the turn in Eugene, Oregon and held off the "100 meter World Record Holder" (at that time) Leroy Burrell to earn the final spot on the World Track and Field Championships team in the 200 meters.

Why, because he met the criteria mentioned above and took the edge on the curve. Athletes who are aggressive in the first 60-70 meters and willing to lay it on the line with **"heart"** are true winners in my book!

Most 200 meter races won or lost by the 150 meter mark. Too often 200 meters runners are ready quit by this point if they are 5-8 meters behind. Athletes who choose to waiting until the final 100 meters and don't "take it on the turn" will never be great 200 meters runners at a Division 1 level. That is what is known as a "high school" strategy/mentality and it doesn't enable an athlete to be in medal contention in major championship races!

In the 2005 Big 12 Outdoor Track and Field Championships held at Kansas State University, my 200 meter runner Tyree Gailes, ran a brilliant technical race and won the championship with a time of 20.57 (FAT) into a negative 1.0 headwind despite having the two pre-meet favorites inside: Nate Probasco, Nebraska's Big 12 Indoor 200 meter Champion and DaBryan Blanton of Oklahoma, the NCAA Indoor 60 meter Champion. Gailes blasted the first 60-70 meters of the turn and made these outstanding athletes quit the race by the 150 meter mark. This strategy took them out of their own race plans and presented Tyree Gailes with his first Big 12 Crown.

The Use of Dorsi-Flexion
Great Sprinting is always done with the use of "Dorsi-Flexion". Dorsi-Flexion is running with the toe and heel up while running. Literally, the athlete is stretching the calf muscle while running.

To run with Dorsi-Flexion, the athlete pulls the heel through to the "buttocks". he/she then places the heel on the ground under the knee. When the athlete lands on the track surface or ground, the foot is then cycled backwards or pulled up to the buttocks. At this point the foot is then brought back down to the ground with again the (toe up) as it makes contact with the ground underneath the knee.

A common mistake made by coaches is telling their athletes to take longer strides. Instead of making the athlete faster, over-striding causes a breaking effect since it causes the athlete to land more often on his/her heel and causes the athlete to lose power.

CURVE RUNNING
Because half of the race is run on the curve it is vital that the athlete know how to run the turn. To master the race, the athlete must learn to "lean" into the curve. To do this the athlete dips the head inwards to the left and at the same time lowers the inside left shoulder. This enables the athlete to "flow" gracefully around the turn instead of trying to "fight" or "outmuscle" the turn. In addition, the

athlete's arms don't cross the mid-point of their body when running the curve. No matter how strong the athlete is, he/she will never win if they fight the curve.

FINAL 100 METERS

When the athlete enters the straight-away for his the final 100 meters, the athlete must be running in the "Hips Tall" position. This position enables the athletes to maximize 100% of his leg power capabilities. During this final stage of the race, it is important that the athlete focus "quick arm" frequency. To have good knee lift, the athlete must maintain a "normal head" position at all times. Once the athlete drops or lowers his head, high knee lift is immediately diminished and stride length starts to shorten. Most athletes try to "over-stride" or "reach" during this final segment which causes them to fatigue or tire faster. In addition it is vital that the athlete keep his/her shoulders and face relaxed during this final period in the race due to the level of lactic acid build-up. When he/she follows these guidelines, a successful finish with a great performance will be theirs.

SAMPLE WORKOUTS

Listed below are some workouts which that are good simulators as preparation for the athlete running the 200 meters:

4 x 100 meter (Curve) **"Fly's"** 20 meter Running start
4 x 60 meter (Curve) **"Fly's"** with 20 meter Running start
5 x 60 meters (Curve) From Starting blocks
4 x 70 meters (Curve) From Starting blocks
4 x 150 meters (Full Curve) From Starting blocks
4 x 100 Meters (Curve) From Starting Blocks

FLY's=Are running starts into the timed distance of 15-20 yards

RACE DISTRIBUTION

Listed below are race splits from the 1993 World Track & Field Championships Stuttgart, Germany. I witnessed this race as the head coach of the Zambia Team and it was truly a great race.

1993 World Championships Stuttgart
(200 Meters-Final)

Athlete	Country	1st 100	2nd 100	200 Final	
1. Frankie Fredricks	NAM	10.39	9.46	19.85	"GOLD"
2. John Regis	GBR	10.28	9.66	19.94	"SILVER"
3. Carl Lewis	USA	10.31	9.68	19.99	"BRONZE"
4. Mike Marsh	USA	10.43	9.75	20.18	
5. Dean Capobianco	AUS	10.36	9.82	20.18	
6. Jean Ch.Trouabal	FRA	10.46	9.74	20.20	
7. Emmanuel Tuffour	GHA	10.60	9.89	20.49	
8. Damien Marsh	AUS	10.62	9.94	20.56	

Have a great track and field season!

Coach Steve Silvey

THE
400
METERS

Race Strategy for the 400 Meters

By

Coach Steve Silvey
Men's Sprints/Hurdles/Relays
Texas Tech University

Based on the times posted in the 400 meters and the 1,600 meter relay by athletes I've coached I feel I can speak with some authority on the topic.

400 METERS		1600 METER RELAY	
Lamont Smith	44.30	Texas Tech University	3:01.69 (2005)
Darnell Hall	44.34	Blinn Junior College	3:01.89 (1994)
Kempa Busby	44.80	University of Arkansas	3:02.02 (2000)
Samuel Matete	44.88	Blinn Junior College	3:02.22 (1994)
Seymour Fagen	44.88	Blinn Junior College	3:02.86 (1992)
Andrae Williams	44.90	University of Arkansas	3:03.14 (2000)

You may be aware that the human body can't sprint an entire 400 meter distance. Scientific studies have shown that the human body can only sprint all out for about 350 meters. Because of this, the athlete must find a point somewhere in the race to "relax" for about 50 meters in the race.

If you break down the 400 meter race into four equal parts, there will be four 100 meter segments. When looking at the races of the great world class 400 meter runners the first thing to notice is that the first 100 meter segment is always the fastest of the four. This is because the human body's "SPEED" energy system is completely fresh at the beginning of the race. No matter how hard the athlete tries to run any of the other four 100 meter segments, the first 100 meter segment will always be the fastest provided an honest effort is being put forth by the athlete.

It is my belief that to be a great 400 meter runner, athletes must have good 200 meter speed along with the strength of an 800 meter runner.

Race Modeling

As preparation for a great 400 meter race, I like to have my athletes do **300 Meter "Event" Runs.**

I break these event runs down into the following zones:

150 Meters: Get out *hard* and "*Attack*" at 90%-95% effort!

151 to 199 Meters: Chill-out and let the momentum that you created during the first 150 meters carry you to the 200 meter mark.

200 Meters to Finish: With the emphasis on cycling the arms quicker and be sure to not over stride or reach. During this final phase to the finish "desire" and "heart" are vital to overcome the lactic acid that often surfaces during this final phase of the race.

How to Time the 300 Meter "Event" Run

I time the first 150 meters and then time the next 50 meter zone and then get a split time for the final 100 meters. Then, I give the athlete a final or total time for the 300 meters. Here is an example:

150 Meters	16.5
50 Meters	6.5
100 Meters	12.5
300 Meters	35.5 seconds

Curve Running

It is important that the athlete is aware of how to run the turn as there are two 100 meter segments in the race or ½ of the race is run on a curve. To master the race, the athlete must learn to lean into the curve. To do this the athlete must dip the head inwards to the left as well as lower the inside left shoulder. This will allow the athlete to "flow" gracefully around the turn with the turn instead of trying to fight or "out-muscle" the turn. The athlete's arms should not cross the mid-point of their body when running the curve. *No matter how strong the athlete is he will never win fighting the turn.*

Late Race Charge

After the athlete relaxes for about 50 meters he must be ready to attack   the final segment of the race by shifting gears one final time. Great 400 meter runners attack from 150 to 200 meters from the finish line.

Athlete's who wait until the final 100 meters and then find a last minute gear, cheat themselves out of running a much faster time. Athletes who attack from 150 to 200 meters out from the finish line are the true champions in my opinion. They are willing to lay it on the line with "heart".

The Final 100 Meters

As the athlete comes of the curve, he must be running in "*Hips Tall*" position. During this final stage of the race it is important that the athlete focuses on great frequency with "*quick arms*" and good knee lift. Most athletes try to "over-stride" or reach during this final segment only to find that they tire even quicker. If the athlete keeps the shoulders and the face relaxed during this period of great lactic acid build-up they will be successful in getting to the finish line with a great time.

Race Splits

As I coach I believe in the high school and the college 400 meter runner running the first and the second 200 meters in the race with 1.50 second differential. World Class athletes should have a differential of between 1.00 to 1.25 seconds.
Here are examples below:

400 METER PACING

First 200 Meters	Second 200 Meters	Final 400 Meter Time
21.5	23.5	44.5
21.75	23.25	45.0
22.0	23.5	45.5
22.25	23.75	46.0
22.5	24.0	46.5
22.75	24.25	47.0
23.0	24.5	47.5
23.25	24.75	48.0
24.0	25.5	49.5
24.5	26.0	50.5
25.0	26.5	51.5
25.5	27.0	52.5

Example Of Proper Pacing:

400 Meter Dash finals

1988 Summer Olympic Games
Seoul, Korea

Place	Athlete	Country	First	200 Second	200 Time	Dif.
Gold Medalist	Steve Lewis	USA	21.41	22.46	43.87	1.05
Silver Medalist	Butch Reynolds	USA	21.68	22.22	43.93	.57
Bronze Medal	Danny Everett	USA	21.37	22.72	44.09	1.35
4th Place	Darren Clark	Australia	21.61	22.94	44.55	.33
5th Place	Innocent Egbunike	Nigeria	21.76	22.96	44.72	1.20
6th Place	Bert Cameron	Jamaica	21.66	23.28	44.94	1.66

We also do numerous drills for the sprinters, hurdlers and relays. I have also published the following materials for junior high, high school and age group track coaches:

- World Class "All Sports" Speed Training program (Book & DVD)
- World Class "Elite" Hurdle Training program (Book & DVD)
- World Class "Essential" Relay Techniques Program (Book & DVD)
- Coach Silvey's "Oregon" Training Program (Book) Complete year of workouts)
- Coach Silvey's Texas Tech Training Program (Book) Complete year of workouts
- The 45 Minute Workout for Middle School & Small HS Program's (Book & DVD)

If you like information on any of these please go to my website:

SSEproducts.com

Good luck in developing your 400 meter runners!
Coach Steve Silvey

200 METER PACE CHART

1st 100 Meters	10.20	10.79	11.05	11.30	11.56	11.82	12.07	12.33
150 Meters	15.00	15.73	16.10	16.48	16.85	17.32	17.60	17.98
2nd 100 Meters	9.80	10.21	10.45	10.70	10.94	11.18	11.43	11.67
Final Time	20.00	21.00	21.50	22.00	22.50	23.00	23.50	24.00

400 METER PACE CHART

100 Meters	11.00	11.63	11.88	12.13	12.38	12.62	12.87	13.12	13.37	13.61	13.86
200 Meters	22.00	22.40	22.87	23.25	23.83	24.30	24.78	25.25	25.73	26.21	26.68
300 Meters	33.00	33.90	34.62	35.34	36.06	36.78	37.50	38.22	38.94	39.67	40.39
Final Time	44.00	47.00	48.00	49.00	50.00	51.00	52.00	53.00	54.00	55.00	56.00

THE

800

METER

RUN

800 METER TRAINING

By
Coach Steve Silvey
The University of Arkansas

Many coaches today consider the 800 meter to be a long sprint event. It is my belief that this athlete to excel must have the speed of a 400 meter runner and the Strength of a 1,500/1,600 meter runner. Some of the 800 meter Runners that I have coached are as follows:

Brandon Rock	Arkansas	1:44.64
Savieri Ngidhi	Blinn College	1:45.50
Simon Kimata	Oregon	1:46.65
Douglas Kalembo	Blinn College	1:46.93
Dennis Stewart	Blinn College	1:47.50
Kenroy Levy	Blinn College	1:48.19
John Good	Blinn College	1:48.37
Ryan Stanley	Arkansas	1:48.86

SPRINT MEDLEY RELAY (200,200,400,800)

Arkansas	2000	3:12.13	Collegiate Record
Blinn College	1993	3:12.67	JUCO RECORD
Blinn College	1992	3:13.45	JUCO RECORD
Blinn College	1992	3:13.91	
Blinn College	1991	3:14.51	

3200 METER RELAY or 4 x 800 meters

Blinn College	1993	7:19.24	JUCO RECORD
Blinn College	1994	7:21.03	
Blinn College	1992	7:22.53	JUCO RECORD
Blinn College	1993	7:23.81	JUCO RECORD-indoors

In this particular article I am going to talk to you about the 400/800 meter runner. While at the University of Arkansas from 1994-2000, I coach a young man named Brandon Rock. Brandon had only 1 year of NCAA eligibility at Arkansas when he was forced to transfer from the University of Nevada-Reno after they dropped their men's program after the 1994 season. Rock entered Arkansas as a 1:47.97 800 meter runner and one season improved to 1:44.91.

Some Brandon Rocks Razorback accomplishments were as follows:

SEC Indoor 800 Meter Champion
NCAA Indoor 800 Meter All-American
SEC Outdoor 800 Meter Champion
NCAA Outdoor 800 Meter National Champion
USA Track & Field National 800 Meter Champion
5th in the 1995 World Championships

What made Brandon Rock so dangerous is that he raced European style in which he would run 50- 51 for the first 400 meters. At 6-3 in height he was a very intimating runner with a long stride. Rock always did a great gob at relaxing from 500 meters to 600 meters in the race and then would crank it up one more time over the final 200 meters. Even though we could never put Brandon into the right situation on the 4 x 400 meter relay, I am a firm believe that with his effortless 22 second 200 meters in practice, Brandon could of run 44.8 if pressed on a relay. Brandon also had another 1:44 year in finishing second in the USA Olympic Trials to Johnny gray and then represented the USA in the 1996 USA Olympic Games in Atlanta., 1997 Rock finished second to mark Everett in the USA Track and field Championships and ran a life time best of 1:44.64.

During the three years that I worked with Brandon Rock, he did a modified cross country program with my boss John McDonnell. This fall training program did not mean cross country races but maybe an occasional 5K road race and several mornings of getting up for easy runs of 3 to 6 miles. This fall base set the tone for a great track and field season as rock ran 1:44 for three consecutive years from 1995 to 1997.

Unfortunately in the fall of 1997, Rock began to think he was superman and no longer thought he needed to listen to his coaches and train hard in the fall or get up in the morning for easy distance runs. In 1998 Brandon Rock became a mere 1:48 800 meter runner. Rock made the same mistake as 1999 and soon lost his sponsorships and his elite running career was over. In 2000 he could not even break 1:50 for 800 meters.

I am big on training structure and the John McDonnell Quote:

"If It Isn't Broke, Then Don't Fix It"

This is why in those bad years of racing for Rock. I told Rock that we are going to do it the same way that we always have or he can coach himself! Rock did and quickly became a average 1:48-1:49 800 meter runners and his elite running career was over. During this time Rock's diet went to crap and he was staying up late at night doing who knows what?

I would like to share with the most amazing feet I ever had with one of 800 meters runners while I was the Head Track and Field Coach at Blinn College. Savieri Ngidhi an 800 meter Runner from Zimbabwe was just unreal at the Texas Relays in 1993! In the morning at 11:30AM, Ngidhi anchored our 4 x 800 meter relay to a JUCO National Record of 7:19.24 with a sizzling 1:45.8 anchor. Then at about 7:00PM the same day Ngidhi anchored out sprint medley Relay to another National JUCO Record of 3:12.67 as we came close to the collegiate record. Savieri's 800 meter anchor was 1:45.5. These two great 800 meter runs were done in a period of less than 8 hours! I am a firm believer that this 800 meter runner does not have to take part in the cross country racing season, but they need to be doing a modified training program with distance runs and lots of hill training. I love hill training for all of my athletes and I am a firm believe that in the fall athletes need to train on softer surfaces and not the track. Even dirt or gravel roads are easier on the body. Athletes don't get hurt running on good grass!

In the fall I love longer intervals on grass from 400 meters to one mile with a slight incline for a hill. The days that we are doing intervals the volume is high and the pace is slow as again we are trying to build strength.

Another Quote from the greatest NCAA Track and Field Coach of All-Time John McDonnell who won 40 NCAA Team Championships at the University of Arkansas is:

"Speed is Strength"

While at the University of Oregon, I coached an 800 meter runner names Simon Kimata. Kimata would run a 4 x 400 meter relay split of low 46 seconds. Kimata ran an occasional mile indoors and he ran a very respectable 4:06.74 indoors off his 800 meter training program. Simon was the 2002 Pac-10 800 meter Champion as well as NCAA Indoor and Outdoor 800 meter All-American for the Ducks.

I believe that the 800 meter runner needs some type of long run from 5 to 9 miles on the weekend and that Mondays should be the hardest day of training for the week. This is because it is the furthest day away from your athlete's next competion. I am a firm believe that:

"Mondays Makes Champions"

Monday should also be the day that the athletes energy systems should be the most fresh from a low key Sunday.

On the next few pages I am going to share with you several sample workouts from various parts of the track and field season. If you would like a complete year Training program this can be found in my Oregon Track & Field Training Book and my "New" Arkansas Training Book which are both a "COOKBOOK" of workouts (September to June). Just adjust the times to your high school runners & your set.

These books can be found on my website: **SSE products.com**

THE
TOTAL
TRACK
&
FIELD
ATHLETE

Developing the Total Track & Field Athlete

By
Coach Steve Silvey
Texas Tech University

The foundation of my track and field training program, which I established years ago, focuses on a very broad base total training program. My training philosophy can help athletes in all sports see the improvements in "SPEED" performance by improvement of the following:

1. Greater Efficiency of Movement (Mechanics)
2. Increase in Flexibility
3. Improve Quickness
4. Better Coordination
5. Increase in Strength
6. Improvement in Techniques

I often hear the statement, "great athletes are born" which is an all-encompassing statement that I cannot agree with. Certainly it is possible for someone to be born with a better "gene pool". From that the likelihood for that person's success is better if those genes are used. However, does that mean that to be a great athlete you have to start with a great gene pool? Absolutely not! Is potential and desire necessary? YES! Our objective as coaches should be to develop a high level of athletic skill in each and every athlete. Why do this? Because the greater the level of athletic skill the athlete possesses the higher the level of sports skill in his particular sporting event. To have the opportunity to experience greatness, athletes have to learn "sport specific skills". Then they have to take the drills and perfect and perform them on a regular basis. By doing this, you become the level of athlete who can excel in any sport you choose!

My objective when developing a great track and field athlete centers around helping the athlete develop his *balance, rhythm, agility, power,* and *flexibility* thru a variety of drills. Great body *balance*, *strength* and *flexibility* equally on both their right and left side of the body are imperative for an athlete to be great. Many athletes will naturally have these qualities on one side of the body, but not on the other side.

As a result they are more prone to athletic injuries on that side of the body because it tends to be weak, awkward, or poorly flexible. Being weak on one side causes the athlete not to reach his/her full athletic potential.

Power is a quality in athletics that is often overlooked by coaches and athletes in their training. For the athlete to increase their power, he/she needs to improve in three main areas:
1. Functional dynamic strength
2. Improve their basic flexibility
3. Improve their speed and quickness

Power is defined as: $$POWER = \frac{FORCE \ X \ DISTANCE}{Time}$$

Force = strength
Distance = a range of motion determined by flexibility
Time = speed or quickness

During the base training of any athlete, a considerable amount of time should be spent on *power training*. To address the need for *power training*, I often devote much of the fall training to doing lots of pre-conditioning on grass hills, stadium stairs and ramps. Much of the preseason work is done in the sand pit with "hurdle-hops" and low-impact "plyometrics". The vast majority of our fall work is on either grass or sand which naturally creates more power and general strength.

Barefoot running is a part of a complete conditioning program. It is useful in order to strengthen the athlete's tendons, ligaments and small muscle groups of the feet. Training shoes act as a cast and do nothing to strengthen the foot.

Leg power is necessary for speed. For an athlete to be able to maximize 100% of his leg power capabilities, the athlete must run "HIPS TALL" over his hips at all times and keep all parts of his body near or under the "center of mass" at all times. I often see many young athletes shrink 3-6 inches while running because they are over-rotating at the hips. This causes a loss of 20%-30% of leg power and a substantial loss in true SPEED performance.

The athlete must also have a tremendous amount of lower leg strength (below the waist) because each time the athlete strikes the ground he is applying three (3) times his body weight to the ground.

The coaching cues when working on proper running mechanics that I use with my athletes on a regular daily basis are:

1. Toe Up
2. Heel Up
3. Knee Up
4. Chest Up
5. Head Up
6. Eyes Up

Most importantly the athletes must remain in "Hips-Tall" position at all times for the 6 coaching cues listed above to be effective. The athlete that does not stay in proper body position over his hips will give up 20-30% of their maximum leg power. This is a common fault of young athletes that have not been instructed properly.

Core Strength is also highly important as it provides a strong foundation for the tremendous forces created by the arms and legs. I am a firm believer that the abdominal area of the body or the core is the control mechanism of the body. Without a strong core the athlete will never become a champion.

SPEED involves the numerous areas of the body - muscle groups, circulation (blood supply to these muscles), the mind and most importantly the central nervous system. As an athlete prepares the body for speed, he/she must develop his/her motor skills so the necessary components for speed are stored as muscle memory.

The Speed Drills and Techniques that I teach my athletes must be learned and perfected at a slow rate of speed first gradually increasing until the athlete can perform them correctly but at faster rate of speed. After the athlete has mastered the drills and techniques, they can increase their range of motion and stride rate.

For an athlete to become fast and stay fast, we must utilize their fast twitch muscles regularly. Have you heard the saying, **"If you don't use it you lose it"**? Well this statement accurately applies to fast twitch muscle fibers.

When it comes to an athlete's SPEED, it starts from the ground up. First, for any athlete to excel in Speed Development, he or she must learn to use "Dorsi Flexion" with his/her foot.   Unfortunately, most young athletes use "Plantar Flexion" instead. "Plantar Flexion" is a BAD habit. Because this downward pointing of the toe causes a breaking effect upon contact with the ground it is similar to continually "riding" the brakes in a moving car. "Plantar Flexion" keeps the athlete's foot on the ground too long, maximizing ground time which translates into slower speed performance. In addition the "braking effect" can put a lot of strain on the ankle, shin, and most of all the hamstring muscles. In my opinion, *"Plantar Flexion"* is the number one cause of "Shin Splints" and Hamstring Injuries.

Hamstring injuries are very common in sports that involve speed. In my opinion the hamstring muscle is the weakest muscle in the body. "Plantar Flexion" increases hamstring weakness. It is important to emphasize strengthening the hamstring muscles one leg at a time as well working on lower back flexibility by spending focused time to strengthen these areas. In addition to the problems caused by "Plantar Flexion" I feel that many hamstring injuries are caused by poor lower back flexibility and this is an area that is often neglected by the athlete.

Great Speed Performance starts with "Dorsi-Flexion". "Dorsi-Flexion" is keeping the toe and heel up while running. The runner is literally stretching the calf muscle while running. When running the athlete pulls the heel tight "through to the buttocks" and then places it on the ground under the knee. When the athlete's foot lands on the track surface or the ground, the foot is then cycled backwards or pulled up to the buttocks. At this point, the foot is then brought back down to the ground with again, the toe up, as it makes contact with the ground underneath the knee. A common mistake made by coaches is to tell their athletes to take "longer strides". "Over-striding" causes a "braking effect" as the athlete often lands on his heel and the athletes also lose *power*.

How does the use of "Dorsi-Flexion" make an athlete faster and why is it better than "Plantar Flexion"? Dorsi-Flexion makes an athlete much more active upon contact with the ground or track and also allows the athlete to "get-off" the ground or track surface quicker. *"Rome was not built in a day"* and don't expect your athletes to pick up this new technique overnight. The bad habits of athletes took years to develop and it will take he/she weeks to correct it, but once the athlete learns "Dorsi-Flexion", the he/she will be much more efficient in landing. Efficient landing minimizes both ground time and air time which translates into faster speed performances.

To run fast an athlete must run on the balls of his/her feet at all times. This means landing on the "widest part" of the front of their foot each and every time. Athletes must also learn how to strengthen the tendons, ligaments and small muscle groups in the foot, ankle and below the knee if they are to be able to run on their toes. An athlete's body cannot be supported unless these areas are strong.

Good exercises to strengthen the feet are,

1. Bare Foot Running
2. Sand-Pit Plyometrics
3. Weight Training exercises focusing below the knee

If an athlete attempts to land and push off their heel, he/she can never master SPEED. **Remember!** Unless you plan on running a marathon *nothing good ever happens on your heel.*

Proper arm action is important for *speed* as well. The athlete must move the arms in a quick and efficient manner stopping the hand near the chin on the upward motion and at the hips on the downward motion. **Remember!** *A short level is a quick lever; a long lever is a slow lever.* To run fast the athlete must have a "Piston" type arm motion to maximize their SPEED! Two key points you should take note are:

1. **The arms never cross the mid-point of the body.** Find the "mid-point" by drawing a line down the middle of your body to separate it into two equal parts. Crossing the mid-point with either the arms or the legs will cause slowing down of SPEED performance because of inefficiency of movement.

2. **The elbows must be kept within 2- 4 inches of the body at all times.** If the arms are too far away from the body, this "Chicken Wing" movement will cause the athlete to lose maximum SPEED performance.

Last but certainly not least, is the posture for the upper body:

1. The shoulders should be kept low and relaxed at all times
2. The face and the jaw should remain relaxed.
3. The athlete's head should remain in its normal position which I refer to as "Neutral Head Position" as if he was merely standing in place.

If the athlete drops his head or eyes slightly when running, it hinders the ability for a nice high knee lift while running. By dropping the head, the athletes now lowers his center of mass causing a domino effect on the rest of his body which in turn causes his performance level to decline. To help the athlete keep his head up, have him raise his eyes and look forward 30-50 yards. Have him focus on an object that is 6-8 feet above the ground that is located past the finish line.

Examples of this would be a tree, building or a set of windows. Doing this ensures that the athlete's head and hips remain tall throughout the entire distance run or the race.

A good diet is vital to achievement. Thankfully athletes are becoming more and more interested in how their diet affects their athletic performance. It is now recognized that the *right diet*, combined with the latest *"legal"* *nutritional supplements* and combined with *proper training, adequate sleep, proper hydration* and *coaching* can significantly improve the overall performance of today's athlete.

I have stated to my athletes many times before, that you can be the greatest trained athlete in the world, but,

Great Training + Poor Eating Habits = Mediocre Performance

Yes, it is true that the talented athlete with a poor diet is going to be at the same level as the athlete who trains only half as hard, yet employs a well-rounded nutritional program.

Good nutrition is about more than just food. Athletes must also drink WATER. Hydrate properly and sufficiently! To be properly hydrated an athlete should be drinking a MINIMUM of 8-10 large glasses (total of 100 oz. +) of water and/or sports drink daily. How do you know if you are drinking enough fluid? If you are sufficiently hydrated, you should be going to the bathroom at least ever 45 minutes during the day and once during the night and the urine is a pale yellow color.

Get Rest! Discipline yourself to get 8-9 hours of sleep each night.

Sleep Facts:
1. Every hour you go to bed before midnight counts as 2 hours of good sleep after midnight.
2. R.E.M. sleep, the deepest of all sleep patterns, can only be achieved when you go to sleep before midnight.
3. Going to sleep before midnight allows your body to have the proper regeneration before the next day's workout.

So, last but not least having been successful as a coach for 25 years, I have developed several products that support a coach's efforts to build a successful team. I encourage you to invest in one of them.

They work for all levels - high school, junior high, club coaches and individuals who work with young athletes.

HOW TO BECOME AN "ELITE" TRACK & FIELD ATHLETE

By
Steve Silvey
Assistant Track Coach
University of Oregon

Listed below are some of the essential items that a young athlete must do to become an "ELITE" Track and Field athlete.

<u>**DO MORE**</u>: Great athletes complete the coach's workouts list then they do more.

<u>**GET REST**</u>: Discipline yourself to get 8-9 hours of sleep each night. Every hour you go to bed before midnight counts as 2 hours of good sleep after midnight. R.E.M sleep, the deepest of all sleep patterns can only be achieved when you go to sleep before midnight. Going to sleep before midnight allows your body to have the proper regeneration before the next day's work-out.

<u>**DRINK WATER**</u>: Hydrate Correctly! You must drink a minimum of 8-10 large glasses of water and sports drink daily. (Total 100 ounces+) How do you know if you are drinking enough fluid? If you are sufficiently hydrated, you should be going to the bathroom at least once every 45 minutes during the day and once during the night.

<u>**EAT TUNA & TURKEY**</u>: Scientific studies have shown tremendous gains in strength levels for athletes when turkey and/or tuna are incorporated into the athlete's diet prior to bedtime. Tuna and turkey contain Tryptophan and other amino acids that aid in establishing deeper sleep patterns.

<u>**EAT FRUITS & VEGETABLES**</u>: Eat plenty of fruits and vegetables every meal. They provided the carbohydrates your body will require to work properly. Eat something GREEN every lunch or dinner-and that doesn't include lime sherbert or lime Jell-O!

POTASSIUM: Eat one or two bananas each morning to ensure that the muscles in your body have enough potassium to endure grueling workouts. If you can't eat banana's then try the legal supplement: Phosphate Plus which can be found at: *SSEproducts.com*

TAKE A CALCIUM/MAGNESIUM SUPPLEMENT: Achieving and maintaining a high calcium level will be very important to your performance as an elite athlete. To increaser the calcium level in you system, you must drink at least one glass of milk, take calcium/magnesium supplements or eat several pints of yogurt daily. Natural muscle contraction cannot occur without a high level of calcium in the system. Low levels of calcium will cause you to have a higher chance of leg cramps and muscle pulls. OSTEO-TECH which can be found at *SSEproducts.com* Athletes who take 1,500mg each day will speed up their recovery from a serious injury!

STRETCH TWICE A DAY: Do you stretching after a warm shower or light jog. When your muscles are warm and pliable, you will get a better, safer stretch. A New type of stretching device the *STRETCH-RITE BELT* (along with a step by step color picture guide) is a great tool that ensures a deep stretch is accomplished without the assistance of a second person.

CARDIOVASCULAR CONDIONING: A more fit person, becomes a better athlete! This means doing a 15-20 minute morning jog or some other form of cross training such as exercise bike or swimming to add to your body's cardiovascular conditioning.

WATCH YOU BODY WEIGHT: Each athlete has an ideal weight to maximize performance. Having just 2-4 additional pounds over your idea body weight can make a difference of 4-6 tenths of a second for every 100 meters you run. This means you are then running at 85% of your potential instead of 100%. A good visual is to imagine you are running with a 2-4 pound backpack on your back. Are you faster with the backpack or without it? Extra weight is no different than carrying a backpack with you all of the time, so to be your best, leave the backpack off-watch your weight!

PROPER RUNNING TECHNIQUE: To become a better, faster runner, many of you must improve your running technique. You must do this Dailey every time you run (morning runs, warm-up runs, and running drills)

Bad habits cannot be changed overnight but over several months an athlete can learn to eliminate those bad habits and replace them with a more efficient running technique.

Running Efficiently=Faster Running Times

POSITIVE MENTAL IMAGERY: Set aside time to visualize your success in your mind each day! Three great times to do this practice visualization:

> ➢ **Prior to going to sleep each night**

> ➢ **Prior to practice each day**

> ➢ **Minutes before a competition**

Paint yourself a very detailed picture. See yourself running your perfect championship race. See yourself winning that race. Hear the crowd. What do you feel when you hear them? How do you feel on the top of the winner's stand. The gold medal is around your neck. Is it heavier than your thought? You're smiling and your picture is being taken. Reporters want to talk to you. What are you feeling? Do you like winning? Are you willing to do what it takes to be the winner you see? Attitude determines altitude. You can have whatever you want if you are willing to work hard and willing to pay the price. What you believe, you will achieve! Always remember: *Positive thoughts bring positive results* ·

In summary, great practice habits translate into great meet performances. When an athlete commits to work hard on a daily basis, he will success and reach his goals on meet day. Nothing worthwhile comes easy. If track and field was easy, there would be no honor or glory in winning! What you put in, time and effort wise, is what you will get out of it. The difference between winners and losers is winners accept the challenge, do what needs to be done to get the job done and leave with the prize, while losers are busy complaining about what it takes to get the job done, the job doesn't get done and they watch the winners leave with the prize. Part-time athletes get part-time results. Zero-time athletes get zero results. Full-time athletes get everything. Which one will you be?

THE
RELAYS

RELAYS

By
Steve Silvey
Assistant Track & Field Coach
Texas Tech University

As we are aware the sport of track and field consists of numerous events but nothing more exciting to watch than the various relay events that are held at each and every track meet. The number of relay events that are contested vary from track meet to track meet.

With regards to the success of a relay team depends on the ability of the "unit" (four athletes) in being able to combine both speed and the ability to pass the stick. Many teams might have superior talent, but unless you are willing to work at passing the stick like clockwork, then you are often no better than the average team that can pass the stick around the entire track efficiently. You must also have athletes that are willing to be coached and told what relay position that are best suited for. Large ego's are not part of the overall success of the relay team. I have also determined some time ago, if the athlete can not take a relay stick then the athlete will either be the lead-off person or will not be part of the relay team at all.

In a nutshell, I want my relay personnel to be able to give and take a stick. I also want my athletes capable of moving to a secondary relay position if needed due to injury. Finally the relay exchanges must be crisp and precise with both athletes at rates near top speed when the exchange is made. Several years ago, I witnessed an High School Track Club (East Cost Classics) that ran under 40.00 (FAT) seconds. What made this so special was the fact that not a single person on the relay unit could run under 10.70 (FAT) for the 100 meters.

Just look at what has happened to the United States teams competing at the World Championships and the Olympic Games over the last decade and you will see our athletes with superior 100 and 200 meter credentials that cannot beat other countries with less talent. It is easy to see why these countries use the same personnel for years and have national training camps at various times during the year to perfect their relay stick passing. How long will take the USA system to get smart enough to adopt a standard relay team instead of using a revolving door method?

I have been very fortune to have produced some outstanding relay teams over the years while I have been at various schools.

Listed below are such relay performances:

400 Meter Relay	**38.97**	**Blinn College**
800 Meter Relay	**1:21.45**	**Blinn College**
1,600 Meter Relay	**3:01.69**	**Texas Tech University**
3,200 Meter Relay	**7:19.24**	**Blinn College**
Sprint Medley Relay	**3:12.13**	**University of Arkansas**
Shuttle Hurdle Relay	**56.29**	**University of Arkansas**

I would like to share with you information to help your relay teams to maximize their true athletic potential.

If you do so desire any additional information Relays, Speed Training, or The Hurdles (110 Hurdles/300 hurdles) you might like to check out these books & video packages. Please refer to the website: **SSEproducts.com**

GENERAL
RELAY INFORMATION

RELAY MARKINGS
All Sprint Relays athletes will use at least two full 42 inch white pieces of tape and construct a "Double Tape Box" to make the best possible visual aid that will allow the outgoing runner to pick up the incoming runner to decrease the chance of error on taking the relay baton.

MAKING YOUR STEPS
Mark off your number of steps from the small International exchange zone marker! Remember that you can use this zone to increase your speed. You still must take the relay baton within the exchange zone!

END OF EXCHANGE ZONE
If you get within 5-6 meters of the end of the exchange zone without still receiving the stick, it is your responsibility as the outgoing runner to slow down slightly to get the stick. This does not mean slam on the brakes though!

THE RELAY STICK TARGET
The outgoing runners must give a high, steady large "V" target to the runner bringing the stick in. The runner should not close their hand until they feel the pressure of the stick firmly in their hand. If the incoming runner misses the first time, he will be able to hit the runner again if you keep the target high, steady and as large as possible! (The key is not to grab for the stick)

400 METER RELAY

Type of Hand-Off:	Non-Visual
Hand off manner:	Right-Left-Right-Left
Number of Steps Given to Incoming Runner:	21 to 25 steps
Box Sizes as of Follows (Double Tape Marks)	Exchange #1 4 steps
	Exchange #2 6 steps
	Exchange #3 4 steps

800 METER RELAY

Type of Hand-off:	Non-Visual
Hand off Manner:	Right-Left-Right-Left
Number of Steps Given to Incoming Runner:	8 Steps
Size of Box for All exchanges	4 Steps

1,600 Meter Relay

Type of Hand-Off:	Use of Visual Hand-offs
Hand off Manner:	Take Stick in Left and then switch
	If needed after leaving zone.

Athletes will always face toward the inside of the track and take off when the incoming runner is 2-3 strides away. The outgoing runner will take three hard steps and then throw back hand with a Large "V" target at the Face level of the incoming runner. The outgoing runner will then look the stick into his hand and once he feels the pressure of the stick, firmly against his hand, he will close it, turn and begin the race.

The athlete may switch the baton to his opposite hand in the next 4-5 strides after taking the stick and safely leaving the congested exchange zone area. The race is on.

SPRINT MEDLEY RELAY (200meters-200 meters-400 meters-800 meters)

Hand Off Manner:	Right-Left-Right (First Three Legs)

Exchange #1	200 meter Man to 200 Meter Man	
	Type of Hand-off:	Non-Visual Hand-off
	Number of Steps:	8 Steps
	Size of Box (Double Tape)	4 steps

Exchange #2	200 Meter Man to 400 Meter Runner	
	Type of Hand-off:	Non-Visual Hand-off
	Number of steps:	8 steps
	Size of Box (Double Tape)	4 steps

Exchange #3	400 Meter runner to 800 Meter Runner	
	Type of Hand-off:	Visual
	(same as 4 x 400 relay)	

4 x 800 Meter Relay
Type of Hand-off   Visual (Same as 1,600 Meter Relay)

Distance Medley Relay
Type of Hand-off: Visual (Same as 1,600 Meter Relay)

Shuttle Hurdle Relay
A relay event in which runners #1 and #3 are at one end of the track, runners #2 and #4 are at the other end of the track. The outgoing runner may leave his blocks when the incoming runner breaks the 1 meter exchange zone plane.

PLEASE NOTE: If any runner leaves early, your team is disqualified!

Back up Procedure: To safe guard against a early departure (Disqualification)
1. The incoming runner yells "GO" as he hits the white 1 meter Tape mark as he is to about to finish the race.
2. The Outgoing runner, while in the blocks, looks out of the corner of his eye, to see when the runner is about to break the 1 meter exchange zone plane.
3. The other runner standing behind the outgoing (runner in the blocks) can also yell "Go" as he sees the runner hit the 1 meter exchange zone plane.

400 Meter Relay
TIME PROJECTION

If you would like to project the time your relay team can run, add up the 100 meter times of your runners from their 100 meter open races and then subtract one of the three category times.

1.)   -3.00   Perfect and Stretched Hand-Offs
2.)   -2.50   Good Hand-Offs
3.)   -2.00   Average Hand-Offs

EXAMPLE:
400 Relay Team   Blinn College 1994

1. Aham Okeke	10.29
2. Ricardo Greenidge	10.38
3. Brian Lewis	10.26
4. Tim Montgomery	10.20
	====
	41.53
	-2.50 Good Hand-Offs
	====
	39.03 Projected Time
	====

National Champions   38.97*** ACTUAL TIME

400 Meter Relay Personnel "Suggestions"

Leg #1   Must be a good starter with great "Natural reaction" (use a hurdler)

Leg #2   Use a tall athlete and perhaps your good 200 or 400 meter runner.

Leg #3   Must be a "Good" turn runner. Great place to use a smaller sprinter.

Leg #4   Fast, but has the "Heart of a Lion" that will fight to the finish line!

Please Note: 200 meter runners will run stronger thru the 400 meter exchange zones and can sustain their top-end speed longer than a 100 meter runner.

1600 Meter Relay Personnel

The following considerations should be used when trying to organize a quality 1,600 meter relay team.

1st Leg- Use a good starter who can run a strong, but a consistent lead-off 400 meters. This lead-off leg is normally a good place to put a 100/200 meter runner that is inexperienced that can pace off of the other 400 meter runners.

2nd Leg-Use a runner who has "GOOD" foot speed that can run a fast the first 100 meters around the turn since this relay use a three turn stagger. A runner with poor foot speed will get your team into traffic problems with the other teams and will lose any good position created by the lead-off runner. This runner must be careful to stay in his or her lane around the first turn (2 Steps on the line=Disqualification) and then cut in gradually towards lane #1 or lane #2 using a tangent. This leg has often been the fastest relay carry (44-45) on my relay teams that have run in the 3:01 to 3:03 range.

3rd Leg- This leg could be your best place to hide a weak leg if your team opened up with two strong legs. Also it could be a good place to place to put your second best 400 meter runner if your team will be behind slightly, so that all of the pressure is not on the anchorman. This is also a great leg to hide your 800 meter runner who is strong but does not have great turnover.

4th Leg- At the anchor position you must have the "Stinger" one who can bring your team from behind if needed or has enough "Intestinal Fortitude" to fight off other teams as they come after you. Normally you will use your teams best 400 meter runner in this position, but if you have the luxury of having two quality 400 meter runners, use the stronger of the two runners as your anchorman. If it comes down to a real race over the last 100 meters, the one who is the strongest physically and has the **"Mentality of a NFL Linebacker",** will often be the one that will pull out the victory for your team!   I am a firm believer that once the speed is gone in the race, it's just a matter who is the strongest and who wants it the most! This is the last event of the track meet so win the 1,600 meter relay and leave the meet on a positive note.

THE
SILVEY
FILE

14 OLYMPIC MEDALISTS

(Coached and/or Recruited by Steve Silvey)

Athlete	Country	Event	Medal

2008 Olympic Games-Beijing

Athlete	Country	Event	Medal
Michael Mathieu	Bahamas	1,600 Meter Relay	Silver
Andrea Williams	Bahamas	1,600 Meter Relay	Silver

2000 Olympic Games-Sydney

Athlete	Country	Event	Medal
Brian Lewis	USA	400 Meter Relay	Gold
Tim Montgomery	USA	400 Meter Relay	Gold

1996 Olympic Games-Atlanta

Athlete	Country	Event	Medal
Lamont Smith	USA	1,600 Meter Relay	Gold
Randy Barnes	USA	Shot Put	Gold
Samuel Matete	Zambia	400 Meter Hurdles	Silver
James Beckford	Jamaica	Long Jump	Silver
Tim Montgomery	USA	400 Meter Relay	Silver
Calvin Davis	USA	400 Meter Hurdles	Bronze
Dennis Blake	Jamaica	1,600 Meter Relay	Bronze

1992 Olympic Games-Barcelona

Athlete	Country	Event	Medal
Darnell Hall	USA	1,600 Meter Relay	Gold
Mike Stulce	USA	Shot Put	Gold

1988 Olympic Games-Seoul

Athlete	Country	Event	Medal
Julius Kariuki	Kenya	3,000 Steeplechase	Gold

OLYMPIANS
Coached and/or Recruited by Steve Silvey)
(36 Athletes & 14 Olympic Medals Won)

Athlete	Country	Year	Event	Medalist
Michael Mathieu	Bahama's	2008	1,600 Relay	Silver
Andrea Williams	Bahama's	2008	1,600 Relay	Silver
James Beckford	Jamaica	2004	Long Jump	
Melvin Lister	USA	2004	Triple Jump	
Tom Montgomery	USA	2000	400 Meter Relay	Gold
Brian Lewis	USA	2000	400 Meter Relay	Gold
Melvin Lister	USA	2000	Long Jump	
Eric Thomas	USA	2000	400 Meter Hurdles	
Floyd Heard	USA	2000	200 Meters	
Samuel Matete	Zambia	2000	400 Hurdles	
Jerome Romain	France	2000	Triple Jump	
James Beckford	Jamaica	2000	Long Jump	
Jean Destine	Haiti	2000	800 Meters	
Samuel Matete	Zambia	1996	400 Meter Hurdles	Silver
Calvin Davis	USA	1996	400 Meter Hurdles	Bronze
Gilbert Hashan	Mauritius	1996	400 Meter Hurdles	
Brandon Rock	USA	1996	800 Meters	
James Beckford	Jamaica	1996	Long Jump	Silver
Jerome Romain	France	1996	Triple Jump	
Andy Kokhanovsky	Ukraine	1996	Discus	
Jean Destine	Haiti	1996	800 Meter	
Lamont Smith	USA	1996	1,600 Relay	Gold
Tim Montgomery	USA	1996	400 Relay	Silver
Judex Lefou	Mauritius	1996	110 Hurdles	
Randy Barnes	USA	1996	Shot Put	Gold
Godfrey Siamusiye	Zambia	1996	3,000 Steeple	
Charles Mulinga	Zambia	1996	10,000 Meters	
Dennis Blake	Jamaica	1996	1,600 Relay	Bronze
Jimmy Peirre-Louis	Mauritius	1996	1,600 Relay	
Henrik Dagard	Sweden	1996	Decathlon	
Mike Francis	Puerto Rico	1996	Long Jump	
Darnell	USA	1992	1,600 Relay	Gold
Mike Stulce	USA	1992	Shot Put	Gold
Samuel Matete	Zambia	1992	400 Hurdles	
Mike Francis	Puerto Rico	1992	Long Jump	
Rico Atkins	Barbados	1992	100 & 200 Meters	
Leo Garnes	Barbados	1992	5,000 Meters	
Anthony Wallace	Jamaica	1992	1,600 Meter Relay	
Ben Koech	Kenya	1992	Long Jump	
Charles Seck	Senegal	1992	100 Meters	
Ian James	Canada	1992	Long Jump	
Alberto Lopez	Guatemala	1988	800 Meters	
Douglas Kalembo	Zambia	1988	1,600 Relay	
Julius Kariuki	Kenya	1988	3,000 Steeple	Gold

WORLD TRACK & FIELD CHAMPIONSHIPS PERFORMERS
(26 Athletes & 18 Medalists)

Athlete	Country	Year	Event	Medalist
Andre Williams	Bahamas	2007	1,600 Relay	Silver
Michael Mathieu	Bahamas	2007	1,600 Relay	Silver
James Beckford	Jamaica	2007	Long Jump	
Andre Williams	Bahamas	2005	1,600 Relay	Silver
Tim Montgomery	USA	2003	100 Meters	
Eric Thomas	USA	2003	400 Hurdles	
James Beckford	Jamaica	2003	Long Jump	
Tim Montgomery	USA	2001	100 Meters	Silver
Tim Montgomery	USA	2001	400 Meter Relay	Gold
Tim Montgomery	USA	2001	60 Meters (I)	Gold
Ramon Clay	USA	2001	200 Meters	
Calvin Davis	USA	2001	400 Meter Hurdles	
James Beckford	Jamaica	2001	Long Jump	
James Beckford	Jamaica	1995	Long Jump	Silver
Brian Lewis	USA	1997	400 Meter Relay	Gold
Brandon Rock	USA	1997	800 Meters	
Brandon Rock	USA	1995	800 Meters	
Calvin Davis	USA	1995	1600 Relay(I)	Gold
Darnell Hall	USA	1995	1600 Relay	Gold
Darnell Hall	USA	1995	400 Meters-(I)	Gold
Jerome Romain	Dominica	1995	Triple Jump	Bronze
Godfrey Siamuisye	Zambia	1995	3000 Steeple	
Charles Mulinga	Zambia	1995	10,000 Meters	
Ryan Hayden	USA	1995	400 Meter Hurdle	
Samuel Matete	Zambia	1995	400 Meter Hurdles	Silver
Samuel Matete	Zambia	1993	400 Meter Hurdles	Silver
Samuel Matete	Zambia	1991	400 Meter Hurdles	Gold
Saveiri Ngidhi	Zimbabwe	1995	800 Meters	
Fabian Muyaba	Zimbabwe	1993	100 Meters	
Jason Hendrix	USA	1993	200 Meters	
Andre Cason	USA	1993	100 Meters	Silver
Andre Cason	USA	1993	400 Meter Relay	Gold
Dennis Mowatt	Jamaica	1993	400 Meter Relay	
Kaphus Lemba	Zambia	1993	400 Meters (I)	
Henrik Dagard	Sweden	1993	Decathlon	
Dennis Blake	Jamaica	1993	1,600 Relay	
Rico Atkins	Barbados	1993	400 Meter Relay	
Seymour Fagen	Jamaica	1991	400 Meters	
Douglas Kalembo	Zambia	1991	800 Meters	
Samuel Matete	Zambia	1991	400 Hurdles	Gold

World Track & Field Championships
18 Medalists

Andre Williams	Silver Medal	2007	1,600 Relay	Bahama's
Michael Mathieu	Silver Medal	2007	1,600 Relay	Bahama's
Andre Williams	Silver Medal	2005	1,600 Relay	Bahama's
Tim Montgomery	Gold Medal	2001	400 M. Relay	USA
Tim Montgomery	Gold Medal	2001	60 Meters-I	USA
Tim Montgomery	Gold Medal	2001	100 Meters	USA
Brain Lewis	Gold Medal	1997	400 Meter Relay	USA
Jerome Romain	Bronze Medal	1995	Triple Jump	Dominica
James Beckford	Silver Medal	1995	Long Jump	USA
Calvin Davis	Gold Medal	1995	1,600 Relay-I	USA
Darnell Hall	Gold Medal	1995	1,600 Relay-I	USA
Darnell Hall	Gold Medal	1995	400 Meters-I	USA
Darnell Hall	Gold Medal	1995	1,600 Relay	USA
Samuel Matete	Silver Medal	1995	1,600 Relay	Zambia
Andre Cason	Silver Medal	1993	100 Meters	USA
Andre Cason	Gold Medal	1993	400 Relay	USA
Samuel Matete	Silver Medal	1993	400 Hurdles	Zambia
Samuel Matete	Gold Medal	1991	400 Hurdles	Zambia

COACH SILVEY

International Coaching Assignments

1996 Olympic Games-Atlanta, Georgia - Zambia Olympic Track Coach

1993 World Track Championships-Stuttgart, Germany - Zambia Track Coach

1992 Olympic Games-Barcelona, Spain - Zambia Olympic Track Coach

USA National Coaching Staffs

1994 USA Olympic Sports Festival Staff (South) St. Louis, Missouri

Junior College Track & Field Hall Of Fame

May 2005-Inductee for Winning 15 National Championships at Blinn College

Elite Athletes Recruited and/or Coached by Coach Steve Silvey

100 METERS

Name	Achievement		University	Time
Andre Cason	SMWC	Recruited	Texas A&M	9.93
Tim Montgomery	JCR/WRH		Blinn College (9.78WR)	9.96
Brian Lewis	OM		Blinn College	9.99
Henry Neal	JUCO Champion		Blinn College	10.07
Stanley Kerr	WJC	Recruited	Texas A&M	10.09
Floyd Heard	Olympian	Recruited	Texas A&M	10.12
Dennis Mowatt	WCP		Blinn College	10.13
Fabian Muyaba	WCP		Blinn College	10.15
Derrick Florence	WJC	Recruited	Texas A&M	10.15
Aham Okeke			Blinn College	10.16
Sammy Parker	NCAA AA		Oregon	10.18
Tyree Gailes			Texas Tech	10.18
Charles Seck			Blinn College	10.24
Derrick Thompson	SEC RU		Arkansas	10.27
Clinton Bufuku			Blinn College	10.28
Kermit Ward			Blinn College	10.29
Kelvin Kelly			Arkansas	10.29

200 METERS

Name	Achievement*		University	Time
Floyd Heard	Olympian	Recruited	Texas A&M	19.85
Ramon Clay			Blinn College	20.03
Stanley Kerr	WJC	Recruited	Texas A&M	20.10
Andre Cason	SMWC	Recruited	Texas A&M	20.11
Jason Hendrix	World Championships		Blinn College	20.25
Derrick Thompson	NCAA-Runner-up SEC Champion		Arkansas	20.31
Henry Neal			Blinn College	20.40
Aham Okeke			Blinn College	20.47
Melvin Lister			Arkansas	20.51
Lawrence Felton			Texas A&M	20.51
Tyree Gailes	Big 12 Champion		Texas Tech	20.57
Trevor Rush			Arkansas	20.58
Dushon Orr			Blinn College	20.59
Ricardo Greenidge			Blinn College	20.61
Andre Williams			Texas Tech	20.66
Brian Lewis			Blinn College	20.70
Kermit Ward			Blinn College	20.71
Tim Montgomery			Blinn College	20.72
Von Brown			Blinn College	20.74
Fabian Muyaba			Blinn College	20.78
Dennis Mowatt			Blinn College	20.79
Michael Mathieu			Texas Tech	20.83
Jordan Kent	NCAA-RC		Oregon	20.86
Windell Dobson			Blinn College	20.87
Chandon O'Neal			Arkansas	20.91
James Dibble			Blinn College	20.92

Elite Athletes Recruited and/or Coached by Coach Steve Silvey

400 METERS

Name	Achievement		University	Time
Lamont Smith	OM (Gold)		Blinn College	44.30
Darnell Hall	WC/OM (GOLD)		Blinn College	44.34
Kempa Busby			Blinn College	44.80
Gil Roberts	WC	Recruited	Texas Tech	44.87
Seymour Fagen	WCP		Blinn College	44.88
Samuel Matete	WC		Blinn College	44.88
Andre Williams			Texas Tech	44.90
Calvin Davis	OM		Arkansas-Ex	45.02
Matt Scherer			Oregon	45.19
Kedar Inico		Recruited	Oregon	45.22
Michael Mathieu			Texas Tech	45.22
Dennis Blake			Blinn College	45.71
Torres Poullard			Blinn College	45.75
Anthony Wallace			Blinn College	45.77
Duane Hill			Blinn College	45.77
Henry Brooks			Blinn College	45.80
Michael Mathieu			Texas Tech	45.90
Ryan Hayden			Blinn College	45.99
Johnny Jacobs			Texas Tech	46.19
Ryan Stanley			Arkansas	46.27
Terry Beard			Texas Tech	46.31
Kevin Baker			Arkansas	46.35
Jonathan Leon			Arkansas	46.37
Albert Booker			Texas Tech	46.45
Brandon Washington			Texas Tech	46.46

800 METERS

Name	Achievement*		University	Time
Brandon Rock	US Olympian NCAA Champion USATF CHAMPION World Championships-5th		Arkansas	1:44.64
Savieri Ngidhi	JUCO Champion		Blinn College	1:45.50
Simon Kimata	PAC 10 Champion		Oregon	1:46.65
Douglas Kalembo	JUCO Champion		Blinn College	1:46.93
Matt Dunn		Recruited	Texas A&M	1:47.19
Dennis Stewart			Blinn College	1:47.50
Kenroy Levy			Blinn College	1:48.19
Errington Lindo		Recruited	Texas A&M	1:48.20
John Good			Blinn College	1:48.37
Ryan Stanley			Arkansas	1:48.86
Manuel Joesph	JUCO Champion		Blinn College	1:49.25
Clevon Clair			Blinn College	1:49.30
Jean Destine			Blinn College	1:49.37
Fitzroy Morrison			Blinn College	1:49.52

Elite Athletes Recruited and/or Coached by Coach Steve Silvey

400 METER HURDLES

Name	Achievement*	University	Time
Samuel Matete	WC (Gold) OM (silver) SMWC (2) JUCO NCH/JCR	Blinn College	47.10
Calvin Davis	OM (Bronze)	Arkansas-Ex	47.91
Eric Thomas	Olympian /JCR/WCP	Blinn College	47.94
Ryan Hayden	WCP	Blinn College	48.37
Samuel Glover	SEC Champion/AA (2)	Arkansas	49.08
Bryan Scott	Big12 Champion (3)/AA	Texas Tech	49.76
Fitzroy Morrison		Blinn College	49.90
Wayne Whyte		Blinn College	49.94
Ralph Carrington	4th World Juniors	Blinn College	50.03
Judex Lefou	Olympian-96	Blinn College	50.08
Marco Morgan	JUCO Champion	Blinn College	50.14
Gilbert Hashan	Olympian-96	Blinn College	50.24
D'Marcus Brown	SEC RU	Arkansas	50.31
Shawon Harris	NCAA-RC/AA	Texas Tech	50.40
Brandon Holliday	PAC 10 Champion	Oregon	50.52
Terry Beard		Texas Tech	50.64
Jansen Hyde		Texas Tech	50.67
AK Ikwauakor	PAC 10 Champion Recruited	Oregon	50.69
Brent Collier		Blinn College	50.70
Shannon Sidney	SEC Champion	Arkansas	50.97

110 METER HURDLERS

Name	Achievement*		University	Time
Eric Mitchum	NCAA-RU		Oregon	13.38
Micah Harris	NCAA-AA		Oregon	13.39
Kevin White	NCAA-Runner-up JUCO Champion		Arkansas	13.41
Marlon Odom	Big 12 Champion (3)		Texas Tech	13.45
Micheal Thomas	NCAA-AA	Recruited	Arkansas	13.49
Marlon Odom	Big 12 Champion (3)		Texas Tech	13.52
Larry Moore			Blinn College	13.53
Shawon Harris	NCAA-AA		Texas Tech	13.60
Rory Norris			Blinn College	13.62
Lawrence Felton			Texas A&M	13.63
Eddie Jackson	SEC RU - Indoors		Arkansas	13.66
Harry Jones	SEC Champion		Arkansas	13.69
D'Marcus Brown	NCAA-AA		Arkansas	13.72
Marco Morgan			Blinn College	13.72
Sean Lightfoot			Arkansas	13.74
Daryl Burgess			Texas Tech	13.78
AK Ikwuakor			Oregon	13.83
Terry Ellis			Oregon	13.93
Judex Lefou			Blinn College	13.97
Omo Osaghe	All-Big 12		Texas Tech	13.99

Elite Athletes Recruited and/or Coached by Coach Steve Silvey

400 METER RELAY

College or University	Year	Achievement	Recruited/ Coached	Time
Texas A&M	1986	AFR	(Recruited Entire Team)	38.63
Texas A&M	1988	NCAA CHAMPIONS	(Recruited Entire team)	38.71
Blinn College	1994	JUCO CHAMPS		38.97
Blinn College	1992			39.16
Blinn College	1994			39.26
Arkansas	2000			39.27
Blinn College	1992			39.30
Blinn College	1991	JUCO CHAMPS		39.31
Blinn College	1992	JUCO CHAMPS		39.35
Arkansas	1998			39.50
Blinn College	1990	JUCO CHAMPS		39.56
Blinn College	1992			39.57
Blinn College	1992	JUCO CHAMPS		39.60

800 METER RELAY

College or University	Year	Achievement* Recruited Coached	Time
Blinn College	1994	JCR	1:21.45
Blinn College	1992		1:21.96
Blinn College	1991		1:22.03
Blinn College	1991		1:22.30
Blinn College	1992		1:22.32
Blinn College	1992		1:22.37
Blinn College	1993		1:22.43
Arkansas	1998	PRRU	1:22.53
Arkansas	1998		1:22.57
Texas A&M	1986	AFR	1:22.59
Blinn College	1993		1:22.67
Blinn College	1992		1:22.68
Blinn College	1990		1:22.83

1,600 METER RELAY

College or University	Year	Achievement*	Recruited/ Coached	Time
Oregon	2005		Recruited Relay Team	3:00.81
Texas Tech	2005	FTW (48Hours)		3:01.86
Blinn College	1994	JCR		3:01.89
University of Arkansas	2000	NCAA-RU		3:02.02
Blinn College	1994	Sun Angel Champs		3:02.22
Texas Tech	2005			3:02.33
Blinn College	1992	TRR		3:02.86
Arkansas	2000			3:03.14
Blinn College	1992	Sun Angel Champs		3:03.25
Blinn College	1992	JUCO Champs		3:03.30
Arkansas	2000			3:03.31
Blinn College	1990	JUCO Champs		3:03.38
Texas Tech	2005	PRRU		3:03.43
Blinn College	1989	JUCO Champs		3.04.05
Blinn College	1991			3:04.23
Blinn College	1990			3:04.27
Blinn College	1994			3:04.64
Texas Tech	2004	ISR		3:04.75

Elite Athletes Recruited and/or Coached
by Coach Steve Silvey

SPRINT MEDLEY RELAY

College or University	Year	Achievement*	Recruited/Coached	Time
Arkansas	2000	CR		3:12.13
Blinn College	1993	JCR		3:12.67
Blinn College	1992	JCR		3:13.45
Blinn College	1992			3:13.91
Blinn College	1991			3:14.51
Arkansas	1995	TRC		3:15.10

3200 METER RELAY

College or University	Year	Achievement*	Recruited/ Coached	Time
Blinn College	1993	JCR		7:19.24
Blinn College	1994			7:21.03
Blinn College	1992			7:22.53
Blinn College	1993	JCR (Indoors)		7:23.81

SHUTTLE HURDLE RELAY

College or University	Year	Achievement*	Recruited/Coached	Time
Arkansas	2001		Recruited entire team	55.28
Arkansas	2000	FTW/PRC		55.37
Texas Tech	2006			55.87
Blinn College	1993	JCR		56.52
Arkansas	1999			56.70
Blinn College	1992			57.29

Elite Athletes Recruited and/or Coached
by Coach Steve Silvey

1,500 METERS

Name	Achievement	College or University	Time
Savieri Ngidhi	National Champion	Blinn College	3:42.64
Leo Garnes	All-American	Blinn College	3;47.82
Quintin John	All-American	Blinn College	3:48.26
Junior Mitchell	All-American	Blinn College	3:48.33
Micah Boinett	All-American	Blinn College	3:49.19
George Tambourides	All-American	Blinn College	3:49.78
Kenroy Levy	All-American	Blinn College	3:49.88
Willy Songok	All-American	Blinn College	3:50.03
Chris Scott	All-American	Blinn College	3:50.42
Richie Dikstaal	All-American	Blinn College	3:51.41
Alberto Lopez	All-American	Blinn College	3:51.50

1 MILE RUN

Name	Achievement	College or University	Time
Savieri Ngidhi	JUCO Champion	Blinn College	4:04.14
Quntin John	All-American	Blinn College	4:06.97

3,000 METERS

Name	Achievement*	College or University	Time
Godfrey Siamusiye	JUCO Champion	Blinn College	8:06.35-I
Micah Boinett	JUCO Champion	Blinn College	8:09.75-I
William Musyoki	JUCO 10K Champ	Blinn College	8:14.87-I
Fallord Moonga	All-American	Blinn College	8:25.82
Charles Mulinga	All-American	Blinn College	8:28.8-H
Danny Kunda	All-American	Blinn College	8:29.25

AA = All American
FTW= Fastest Time in the World
NCAA-AA = NCAA All American
OGM = Olympic Gold Medalist
PRRU = Penn Relays Runner-Up
Championships
TRC = Texas Relays Champion

AFR = All Freshman Record
ISR = Indoor School Record
NCAA-RC = NCAA Regional Champion
OM = Olympic Medalist
SEC RU – SEC Runner-Up

TRR = Texas Relays Record

CR = Collegiate Record
JCR = Junior College Record
NCAA-RU = NCAA-Runner-up
PRC = Penn Relays Champion
SMWC = Silver Medalist at World

WC = World Champion

Elite Athletes Recruited and/or Coached by Coach Steve Silvey

3,000 METER STEEPLECHASE

Name	Achievement	College	Time
Micah Boinett	JUCO Champion	Blinn College	8:27.74
Godfrey Siamusiye	JUCO Champion	Blinn College	8:38.64
Willy Songok	JUCO Champion	Blinn College	8:48.70
Junior Mitchell	All-American	Blinn College	8:59.09
Danny Kunda	All-American	Blinn College	9:01.05
Leo Garnes	All-American	Blinn College	9:07.90

5,000 METERS

Name	Achievement*	College	Time
Godfrey Siamusiye	JUCO Champion	Blinn College	13:56.09
Ludvig Edman	JUCO Champion	Blinn College	14:15.04
Fallord Moonga	All-American	Blinn College	14:23.37
Charles Mulinga	JUCO 10K Champ	Blinn College	14:24.31
Willy Songok	JUCO Champion-I	Blinn College	14:29.52
William Musyoki	All-American	Blinn College	14:29.82
Damian Curtis	All-American	Blinn College	14:36.24
Danny Kunda	All-American	Blinn College	14:41.57
Herbert Habyarimana	All-American	Blinn College	14:41.62
Leo Garnes	All-American-1,500	Blinn College	14.45.68

10,000 METERS

Name	Achievement*	College	Time
Godfrey Siamusiye	JUCO Champion	Blinn College	29.25.60
Ludvig Edman	JUCO Champion	Blinn College	29:46.46
Fallord Moonga	All-American	Blinn College	29:52.94
Charles Mulinga	JUCO Champion	Blinn College	30.07.91
William Muysoki	JUCO Champion	Blinn College	30:33.25
Berhane Reddy	All-American	Blinn College	30.48.20

AA = All American
FTW= Fastest Time in the World
NCAA-AA = NCAA All American
OGM = Olympic Gold Medalist
PRRU = Penn Relays Runner-Up Championships
TRC = Texas Relays Champion
WCP =World Championships Performer

AFR = All Freshman Record
ISR = Indoor School Record
NCAA-RC = NCAA Regional Champion
OM = Olympic Medalist
SEC RU – SEC Runner-Up

TRR = Texas Relays Record
WJC = World Junior Champion

CR = Collegiate Record
JCR = Junior College Record
NCAA-RU = NCAA-Runner-up
PRC = Penn Relays Champion
SMWC = Silver Medalist at World

WC = World Champion
WRH = World Record Holder

Coach Steve Silvey

A veteran at the national and international level for over 25 years and coaching 28 collegiate national champion squads, and numerous All-Americans and 14 Olympic Medalists and 17 World Championships Medalists at several of the nation's most prestigious programs.

At the international level, Coach Silvey served as the **Zambia Olympic Coach for Track and Field** in the 1992 and 1996 Olympiads, and produced its first ever Olympic medal in the sport of track and field with Samuel Matete in the 400 hurdles (silver medal). Silvey also served as the head coach for Zambia at the 1993 World Championships in Stuttgart, Germany as Samuel Matete again won the World Championship Silver Medal.

Among the 14 Olympic Medalists Silvey worked with, Samuel Matete (47.10) and Calvin Davis (47.91) won Silver and Bronze medals respectively in the 400 meter hurdles in Atlanta in 1996 while he has also coached 15 World Championship Medalists. Samuel Matete was also the 1991 World Champion in the 400 meter hurdles as well as silver medalist in 1993 and 1995.

Silvey has also coached and recruited Olympic sprinters Tim Montgomery (9.78), Brian Lewis (9.99), Olympic 4 x 400 relay gold medalists Lamont Smith (44.30) and Darnell Hall (44.34) Hall was also the 1995 World Indoor champion at 400 meters. Silvey also coached 2000 Olympian and 400 meter hurdler Eric Thomas (47.97) Montgomery set the World Record in 2003 for the 100 meters with his 9.78 clocking.

At the World Junior Championships level he coached one champion at Blinn College (Ralph Carrington, 1,600 meter relay) and recruited four at Texas A&M (Derrick Florence 100 meters; Stanley Kerr 200 meters; Percy Waddle 1,600 meters Relay, Andre Cason, 100 meters).

Silvey who was inducted as a coach into the National Junior College Hall of Fame (2005) has an unique quality of having won 19"Team" championships in the SEC, Big-12 and PAC-10 conferences. Individually, his resume boasts over 500 All-American awards, 26 World Championship Competitors and 34 Olympians.

Silvey served as Recruiting Coordinator and Assistant Track Coach for Texas Tech University from 2004 to 2007. While with the Red Raiders, Silvey Helped lead the 2005 men's outdoor team to it's first ever Big-12 Conference "Team" Championship. Silvey's sprinters, hurdlers and relays scored over 100 of the 149.50 points that won the schools first ever Big-12 championship for the Red Raiders.

The 2007 men's outdoor track team also finished as Big 12 Runner-up this past season. Silvey's impact on **Texas Tech University** resulted in 9 new school records during his 3 years with the Red Raiders.

In 2007 alone Silvey coached senior Marlon Odom to 60M hurdle and 110M hurdle school records, Big 12 Titles, NCAA Regional Title and All-American accolades. He coached senior Bryan Scott in the 400 meter hurdles earning a Big 12 Title, NCAA Regional Crown and NCAA All-American status. Two of Silvey's athletes Andréa Williams and Michael Mathieu also won silver medals as members of the Bahamas 4 x 400M relay at the 2007 World Championships in Japan and added a Pan-American Games Championship.

During the 2006 season, Silvey hurdlers tallied five All-American honors and set four school records. Shawon Harris earned All-American accolades in the 60 hurdles, 4 x 400 relay (Indoors) and the 400 meter hurdles. Odom and Scott each received the honor during the outdoor season, with Odom's in the 110M hurdles and Scott in the 400M hurdles. Silvey also coached both Shawon Harris (400H) and Marlon Odom (110H) to NCAA Mid-West Regional Championships

During his first season in Lubbock, Silvey saw his athletes earn 12 indoor all-conference Honors, one indoor conference title(Andre Williams, 600Y), five indoor All-American plaques, 21 outdoor all-conference honors, three outdoor conference champions Tyree Gailes(200M) Marlon Odom(110H) and Bryan Scott (400H) and six outdoor NCAA All-American Honors.

Sprinter Tyree Gailes was the Big 12-conference runner-up in the 100 meters (10.36) In the 400 meters, his athletes took second, third, fourth and sixth place finishes accumulating 22 points for the team total. In the 400 meter hurdles he guided three of his athletes to top five finishes, totaling 23 points. His athletes set three indoor school records, one ATC record and four outdoor school records, as members of 2005 Big 12 Team Champions. Silvey's athletes accounted for over 100 points on the way to 149.50 points and their first track and field "Team" title in school history.

Andre Williams also earned a bronze finish in the 400 meters (44.90) at the NCAA outdoor Championships Williams was also a member of the 4 x 400 meter relay team that clocked a school record breaking time of 3:01.89 a world best at the time.

While at the **University of Oregon** from 2001-2003 Silvey made a quick impact on a struggling program as during Silvey's first year the Men's team jumped from 5th place to 2nd place at the 2002 PAC-10 Outdoor championships. In Silvey's final season with the Ducks, the Men's Team claimed the 2003 PAC-10 Championship- an accomplishment not seen in 12 years. Silvey's to solid recruiting classes also produced another PAC-10 Conference Championship in 2005 and a 3:00.81-1,600 meter for the Ducks.

In 2003 the Ducks lead by a heavy freshman recruiting class, sent six sprint and hurdle entries to the NCAA Championships along with a relay team., to go along with a pair of NCAA West Regional Champions and 9 top 9 finishes at the Pac-10 Championships Silvey Coached Sammie Parker to a fifth-place finish at the NCAA Final and was the NCAA Regional champion with a season best of 10.18. Parker also finished third in the 2003 NCAA Indoor Championships with an Oregon school record of 6.62 for the 60 meter dash. Also 18 year old freshman hurdler, Eric Mitchum became the PAC-10 runner-up with a time of 13.73 and was beaten only by eventual NCAA Champion Ryan Wilson of USC. In 2004 Eric Mitchum was the NCAA Outdoor Championships runner-up with an Oregon school record of 13.38.

During the 2002 season with the Ducks featured a pair of NCAA All-Americans - 110 Meter hurdle school record holder Micah Harris (13.67) and 800 meter runner Simon Kimata. At the PAC-10 Championships Simon Kimata won the PAC-10 800 title and Brandon Holiday captured the PAC-10 400 Meter Hurdle Championship with his (50.73) clocking. Micah Harris was also the PAC-10 Runner-up in the 110 Hurdles.

At the 2002 NCAA level, Harris took seventh in the NCAA final (13.78) while Kimata added fifth place indoors (1:49.56) and ranked third-fastest outdoors among collegians at season end (1:46.65). In his season debut indoors, sprinter Sammie Parker finished fourth in the NCAA Championships in the 60 meter dash (6.66) after having posted a school record of 6.63 in the prelims.

Prior to his arrival in Eugene, Silvey built his reputation at two of the nations top track and field programs-The University of Arkansas and Blinn College-in which he was a part of 28 NCAA national team championships, including a stretch of 13 straight years before leaving the Razorbacks after the 2000 outdoor campaign.

As the Sprints/Hurdles/Relays mentor at the **University of Arkansas** from the fall of 1994 through the 2000 outdoor season, he was part of 13 NCAA indoor and outdoor track & field and cross country team titles and 17 SEC "TEAM" Championships. His athletes won 15 All-American honors (including one NCAA champion and three NCAA runner-up) and 13 outdoor track and field SEC individual titles.

The 2000 season was perhaps the finest by his athletes who posted one of the nations top times in the 4 x 100 relay (39.27), a collegiate record in the sprint medley relay (3:12.13), took second in the NCAA 4 x 400 Final (3:02.02), and won the prestigious Penn Relays. Shuttle relay in the fastest time in the world that season with (55.37) among his individuals, DeMarcus Brown was an All-American in the 110 hurdles and owned a collegiate best of 13.72-one of three Hogs that ran 13.75 or faster that year under his guidance-while All-American 400 Hurdler Samuel Glover owned a best of 49.08.

Also at the NCAA Level, he coached 800 meter Champion Brandon Rock (1:44.64) who made the 1996 U.S. Olympic Team, and a pair of national runner-up – 110 meter hurdler Kevin White (13.41) and 200 meter sprinter Derrick Thompson

(20.31) Presently Silvey coached athlete's still hold 5 University of Arkansas school track and field records.

Prior to arriving in Fayetteville, he coached was five time national coach of the year at **Blinn College** as his squads won 15 national Championships in seven years. At the Brenham, Texas institution, Silvey produced 164 All-Americans, 128 individual national champions and 27 relay champions. His cross country program added a national championship 1993 and another in 1994 only 6 weeks after he departed for Arkansas, while his 1992 indoor and outdoor squads set the record for most points at the national Junior college championships indoors (288) and outdoors (263). Track and Field News rated his recruiting classes best in the nation from 1989-93 a first for a junior college.

Silvey's 1992 and 1993 Blinn College teams were voted the "Outstanding Team" at the Texas Relays and the 1992 team also added the crown of "USA Men's National Relay Ranking Champions" according to Track and Field News. In 1993 Silvey's team was honored as the nations "Top Dual Meet" Track Team according to Track & Field News.

Prior to his stint at Blinn, Silvey served as men's and women's assistant track coach and recruiting coordinator at **Texas A&M University** from 1984 to 1987. Silvey helped position the Aggies rise to national prominence, as A&M finished among the top six NCAA men's squads twice during his stay (sixth in 1986 and 1987). Silvey's star-studded recruiting classes at Texas A&M included world class track athletes such as 200 meter Olympian Floyd Heard, 1993 World Championships 100 meter silver medalist Andre Cason, and Olympic shot put champions Randy Barnes (1996) and Mike Stulce (1992). Silvey's Three star studded recruiting classes produced so much bang that in 1989 the Texas A&M University Aggies lost the NCAA Championship by a mere 2 points to LSU!

Silvey Also spent five years coaching on the high school level in Iowa, Houston, Texas and Louisiana. Silvey help produce two Texas Relays Champions in high jumper, Ken Carter (6-10) and sprinter, Tony Jones (10.32) while at Sam Houston High School in Houston. Jones was ranked the #1 High School 100 Meter sprinter in the Nation by Track and Field News in 1983.

A 1980 graduate of Truman State University (Kirksville, Mo) with a bachelor's degree in environmental science education, he added a master's degree from Texas A&M University in physical education in 1987.

Lone Star "Elite" Track & Field Clinic

Do you want to become a better Track and Field Coach? Then you need to attend an **"A" level** clinic each year!

The Lone Star Elite Track and Field clinic, which originated in 2004, always has some of the nation's top high school and college coaches speaking such as:

> - Tony Veaney-Ex UCLA Coach
> - Boo Schexnayder-Ex LSU Coach
> - John McDonnell-University of Arkansas
> - Fred Harvey-University of Arizona
> - Jeremy Fisher-USA Olympic Training Center

Save the date on your calendar -- it is now always held the *Second Weekend of December* in Dallas, Texas. We have speakers and events taking place on both Friday afternoon & all day Saturday. We typically have coaches from a 5-6 state region. It is a fun, informative way enabling you to fulfill 15 hours of Continuing Education that is required by your state. We also have a fun Coaches Social on Friday night.

The clinic brochure & additional information will be posted on our website 5-6 months before the clinic at:

SSEproducts.com

E-mail: Coach Steve Silvey for a Clinic brochure at: WCspeed@hotmail.com

The Lone Star "Elite" Track & Field Clinic is the Best Track & Field Clinic in the South!

DO YOU NEED A
DVD
SHOWING THE VARIOUS DRILLS IN THIS BOOK?

1. SPRINT DRILLS-DVD

2. HURDLE DRILLS-DVD

3. RELAY DRILLS-DVD

Go to: *SSEproducts.com*

2773779R00111

Printed in Great Britain
by Amazon.co.uk, Ltd.,
Marston Gate.